The Book

of

Rest

The odd psychology of doing

nothing

A. J. Marr

"Art Marr's amusing and thoughtful analyses of psychology have long delighted readers of his books and blogs. Now his 'The Book of Rest' gives an engaging antidote to perseverative thought and stress. Marr is always a good read."

Dr. Kent Berridge, James Olds Distinguished University Professor of Psychology and Neuroscience at the University of Michigan

Preface

Or, why you don't need to read this book

How to Rest Deeply

Take your watch, mark the time, do and/or think of your meaningful tasks at hand or in the future, and simply avoid *all* perseverative thought (distraction, worry, and rumination) for each of the hours that you will perform these tasks. See if you can do that for two or three consistent hours a day, and merely record your progress over a few days. Your muscles will soon be at an inactive or resting state, and their prolonged inactivity will result in the release of opioids or 'endorphins' in the brain that will give you a strong feeling of pleasure. In other words, *persistent relaxation induces a positive and natural narcotic state*. You will note that you will feel totally relaxed and have greater self-control and an accompanying sense of positive arousal or alertness, thus representing good feelings and much higher productive capacities that will extend into your otherwise stress filled day. *(a summary explanation of this is on p.39)* And the good thing is that you will be fully rested and alert and experience a natural 'high', and will not have to take a course on mindfulness, or meditation, or even for that matter read the book that follows! It's that simple.

So what's new about this procedure?

Nothing really, as it is embedded in all meditative procedures, which in common practice also require you to avoid all perseverative thought for a set period. Deep rest simply takes time, and meditation in all its variants (yoga, mindfulness, focal meditation) is the one resting procedure that fully accommodates this requirement. The difference is that meditation adds wholly extraneous behaviors like mumbling nonsense words, focusing on your belly button, climbing mountains in Tibet, or otherwise isolating yourself from your daily activity and decision making, which cannot be kept up for a long period because it's downright boring. That's good for the folks who sell meditation to you, but not so good for the average Joe who can ill afford to waste time.

What is new is that the procedure can be a part of your daily activity and help you be much more productive and feel great. The book attempts to provide an explanation as to why the procedure works, and explanations are needed not only to justify behavior, but they also need to be easily falsified, which is what the failure of this procedure would promptly do. Unlike taking untested medicines, going to a mountain retreat, or buying life insurance, there is no danger, no inconvenience, and no out of pocket expense for trying the procedure. It works or it does not, and you'll know this quickly.

If the procedure works, then reading the explanation that follows is superfluous. If it doesn't work, the explanation is wrong. Either way is reason enough for you not to read the book. But you can go ahead anyway if you are curious.

Introduction

Relax!

It's easier than you think!

A state of rest or relaxation is the one emotional state (and it *is* an emotion by the way) that we want to accompany us always. It is a source of energy, resilience, happiness, and pleasure. There are a million ways to relax, or so it seems, but no one explanation of what relaxation is, how it works, and what makes the muscles tense, or relax. In its simplest guise, it's merely a state of inactivity, in effect the act or non-act as it were of doing nothing. But what is doing nothing? What is its psychology, its philosophy, its *explanation*?

You see, without a suitable explanation, you will never learn how to relax or be motivated to be relaxed because your methods will be ill informed, uncertainly justified, confused, time consuming, and for the most part, ineffective. Proceeding from explanation, you can learn how to be relaxed, why it is important, do it simply and easily, and in the bargain, know whether your explanation is up to snuff, or not.

That indeed is what good explanations do. They provide the means to test them, the procedures that vindicate them, and self-destruct or morph into better explanations if they don't. If they work they provide a window to the world, and if they don't, then it pays for the people like me who propose them not to quit their day job. Good explanations also act to compress a world of facts within a phrase, and from the seed of a simple idea see emerge a universe of possibilities. From Pasteur's theory of disease to Darwin's principle of natural selection to Einstein's $E=MC^2$, good explanations are simple, easy to understand, and above all make firm and bountiful predictions that are easy to test.

So, following this hallowed tradition, I will propose a simple explanation of relaxation and its antithesis of stress that is entirely new and contrarian to the common view that posits them as an artifact of a certain prehistoric relationship with lions, and tigers, and bears. I will also break with scientific tradition by presenting my argument in backwards order, which is from the procedure to the explanation rather than the opposite. This is after all a self-help book first. So, we will get on with the self-help part, and with its practical success, hopefully the reader will have some interest into *why*.

Chapter 1

A Get Rest Quick Plan

Here is the fool proof method to being relaxed, staying relaxed, anywhere and anytime. No seven-day seminar, doctor's appointment, or heavy lifting is required, and you can even skip the rest of this book. It consists of three words. Read it slow so that it can sink in. The explanation that follows is easy too, and it is hoped, self-evident.

Avoid Cognitive Perseveration

That's it. Sounds great, and it seems simple too. Let's get started, you say. One thing though.

What the heck is cognitive perseveration?

Cognitive perseveration is what you tend to *not* do when you are walking on the beach, are at home sitting on an easy chair looking at your garden, or are otherwise unbothered by the worries, cares, and distractions of the world. In these occasions, relaxation is the order of the day. That's because cognitive perseveration *is* the worries, cares and distractions of the world, and that's what's causing you to be tense or 'stressed'. Cognitive perseveration is consciously (e.g. worry, rumination) or non-consciously (e.g. apprehension, distraction) dwelling on decisions, problems, or dilemmas that have no positive resolution. To avoid these cognitive events, the common solution is to physically remove ourselves to a secluded spot, but is this necessary? After all, perseverative thoughts are merely cognitive behavior, and you can pretty much avoid them at will, or can you?

You can, if you have the proper justification, born of explanation. But first, let's define what we mean by worry, care, and distraction. It all has to do with indecision, dealing with dilemmas, or more specifically, our inability to make a decision in foresight or hindsight when we know we must. Can't figure out God's opinion of you or comprehend your income taxes? Relax, you can just postpone it for another time. However, if you are near death or tax time, death and taxes take a whole new meaning, and you need to make some good decisions now.

Cognitive dilemmas that reflect continuously considering past, present, and future events are respectively called rumination, distraction, and worry. These dilemmas have no satisfactory issue, and likely never will, but we keep at them until we are tense and miserable. To illustrate, let us conduct a simple mind experiment, which is way of translating the hypothetical into the obvious.

On your way to work, you accidentally back over your cat, and he is on his way now to the animal hospital to recuperate. Naturally you are upset about this, and are somewhat tense too as your mind is set off in different ways, none of them good. So, you ruminate or mull over the decisions you could have made to avoid the accident, worry about your wife's reaction and how you will respond, and are distracted enough to call the hospital every few minutes to check on the health of your beloved tabby. These represent cognitive dilemmas that leave you no recourse. In this case, thinking about what decisions you could have made, will make, or will make now are fruitless, with taking any fork in the road leaving you as miserable as before.

The solution is simple, merely avoid or otherwise eliminate these perseverative thoughts *completely and consistently*, and you will be calm and relaxed.[1] However, it is a common aspect of our thought that we feel we have no choice but to worry, fret, and be distracted, if not constantly than often enough to disturb the inner calm which is the default state of being alive. We in other words justify to ourselves that there is nothing we can do but muddle through the slings and arrows of inevitable self-inflicted misfortune, a justification that is flat wrong.

As we shall see, faulty justifications come from faulty explanations. Fix the explanation and the motivation to change becomes real because we now know how our stresses work. Knowing yourself is the essence of philosophy, and to be able to rest, we must be philosophers as well.

---

[1] And very likely you will be happy too, since persistent relaxation (a relaxed state for a half hour or more) is an affective state because it increases the level of endogenous opioids centered in the midbrain, which are the cause of all our pleasures, and mitigates the palatability or reward value of other behaviors (food, alcohol) that increase opioid release. In this way it inhibits otherwise harmful cravings. Perseverative cognition may also be defined as a type of 'mind wandering', which has as of recent been strongly correlated with a state of unhappiness. For more on this, look at the TED video by the psychologist Matt Killingsworth.

Chapter 2

Rest Explained

Rest is simple to explain, it's nothing really, or to be exact, doing nothing. Rest is a matter of generalized muscular inactivity, and its benefits are manifest. To be rested or relaxed means to refrain from perseverative thought, which means that without worry, rumination, and constant distraction, you are less likely to be frustrated, depressed, or angry. Working in a rested state leads you to be more productive, focused, and less easily tired. Rest also feels good or is pleasurable because muscular relaxation is accompanied by the continuous release of 'endogenous opioids' in the brain.[2] These naturally occurring brain chemicals help reduce blood pressure, indirectly strengthen the immune system, reduce our sensitivity to pain, reduce addictive cravings for other substances

---

[2] And if you concur with the Epicurean belief that a state of happiness is equivalent to a state of continuous pleasure, then the continuous opioid release in relaxation is just your ticket. Opioids are the source of all of our pleasures, from eating a ham sandwich and smelling a rose to having sex, but whereas our common pleasures end with satiety, the opioid induced pleasures of relaxation can continue without end as long as we stay relaxed. Although opioid inducing drugs are addictive, it must be noted that the positive affective states associated with other psycho-active substances or behaviors, whether it be for addictive drugs (heroin, cocaine) or video games or the 'pleasures' of esteem, power, of affiliation activate not opioid but *dopamine* systems in the brain that instigate action, not sustain repose. This state of 'wanting', although positive, is not pleasure, any more than an itch that demands to be scratched. Sounds confusing? It needn't be, and for more information that can sort this all out for you, I refer you to this article by the neuropsychologist **Kent Berridge**, whose work firmly established that our pleasures, or what we like and want, are not quite what we think they are. http://www.ncbi.nlm.nih.gov/pmc/articles/PMC2756052/

that increase opioid levels (food and alcohol), and makes your brain work better.

Good stuff indeed. So why don't we feel rested all the time? The short answer is because we can't make up our mind, and our musculature is called upon to help us do so, but in a quite unexpected way. The cost is the loss of all the benefits of relaxation, for the prospective gains that as will be demonstrated, are often utter mirages.

So, that brings us to explaining the converse of relaxation, or muscular tension. Our muscles move when we walk and talk and grasp things, and they also tense and are primed to move when we are about to engage in a strenuous activity, from running a marathon to running away from a predator. For these voluntary muscles, they continue being activated when they tire, and when they start to hurt we stop. Whether running, talking, grasping, or lifting, we have a conscious control over these aptly named 'voluntary' muscles, and cease their activity before we approach total exhaustion. However, there is another class of muscles which hold us up. These muscles are moving all the time, and often for reasons so slight that they are barely if at all perceived. These are our postural muscles. When they activate we scarcely perceive it, and only when they remain activated do we remark upon it, as they leave us literally exhausted and in pain. These are our 'involuntary' muscles that act reflexively and non-consciously, for the most part that is, and how and why they work is the pivotal concern of this book.

To illustrate, take a relaxing drive to the beach, say the destination is a three-hour drive away. You walk on the beach, you swim, and when you come back you are exhausted. So why are you so tired? That's because your postural muscles are continually activated, adjusting your torso to every twist and turn, bump and dip in the road. All that muscular adjustment is pretty darn tiring, and your relaxing trip ends up anything but.

But there are also non-physical or 'mental' reasons that lead to the sustained activation of these muscles. These reasons are generally non-conscious in nature, yet cannot be easily explained or 'verbalized'. Now, acting non-consciously is no mystery to us, as we can always explain it in retrospect. Drive your car to work in the morning, and your conscious attention can be directed to the radio, a phone call, or day dreaming, and yet non-consciously you are making continuous and rational decisions to speed up, slow down, make turns, and keep on course to your destination. Your muscles move to steer the car because of rational opportunities that are taken moment by moment to get you places in the safest and quickest way, and you can easily rationalize or understand them after the fact.

But what happens if opportunities conflict, with no satisfactory recourse of choosing one over the other, and much to lose if one route is chosen over the other? Dallying over such dilemmas is not a productive thing, and to force you to make your decision quickly or else retreat from the dilemma altogether, your body sends you another non-conscious message. Namely, your postural muscles contract, soon tire, and the resulting discomfort forces you to attend to the problem and make a decision, or else escape the situation. This brings us to the pivotal concept of this book that is at the core of our procedures and explanation.

Voluntary muscles move because of opportunities, and involuntary muscles move because of dilemmas.

In the tale of Buridan's Ass, an ass is faced with the dilemma of being equidistant from a bale of hay and a bucket of water. Not being able to decide whether to eat or quench its thirst, the ass simply starved to death as it pondered the unresolvable. As humans who daily encounter far more dilemmas than an ass could possibly perceive, it is equally understandable that we would hesitate, and in the aggregate, lose our days rather than lose our lives. Of course, we would not starve ourselves to death for any one choice, but add up all those micro-costs for those countless albeit small dilemmas we face daily, and we might as well starve to death in face of a day's indecision.

Whereas nature abhors a vacuum, human nature abhors the vacuum of indecision. For the minor indecisions that populate our working day, there is rarely a threatening event that would cause us to take flight or fight, and they certainly aren't demanding in the sense of a pending deadline at work. They are minor, trivial events, but they are persistent, and that is the key. They cannot be ignored, and they cannot be acted upon either, and since thinking is of little use in resolving them, your postural muscles contract to expedite your thinking for you, and force you to make a choice or avoid the situation. So why do postural muscles contract to begin with when you are posed with dilemmas? It is because they *hurt*. But what is the purpose of pain? Simple. Pain signals the problem and its obvious remedy, namely avoidance. Think about it. We don't put our hands on hot cooking pots, roaring fires, or hornet's nests because these things will hurt, and if we didn't have a sense of pain to warn us when we touch hot things, then instead of being able to make toast, we would *be* toast. Pain makes a faster case for action than deliberation, and our minds oblige our need to survive by forcing us to make a choice or avoid the situation. This avoidance can be physical or mental, as we can walk away from the situation or just avoid thinking about it. In general, you don't want to think about events that cause pain, and if pain makes your decision making speedier and more useful or else impels you to escape, it has survival value and is thus easily learned. [3]

---

[3] As with nearly all theories that are purportedly worth their salt, our theory is not original, but was conceived by the psychologists Neal Miller and John Dollard in the 1950's. Their Dollard-Miller theory of anxiety hypothesized that tension and anxiety (or fear, which they broadly defined as a pain reaction to conditioned stimuli) were secondary or learnable 'drives' that occurred whenever one was faced with 'choice-choice' conflicts, and to escape these continuous or perseverative conflicts, anxiety impelled faster avoidance behavior, and was reinforced. For example, *avoidance-avoidance* conflicts would represent a conflict between two choices we would rather avoid, such as visiting the dentist or living with an aching tooth. *Approach-approach* conflicts represent conflicts between two desirable options, such as conflicts between whether to access social media or stay focused on work. Finally, *approach-avoidance* conflicts represent conflicts between options

So for example, on April 1 we think about our taxes, feel tense when we see no good alternative to paying up, and because of the pain postpone our day of reckoning until April 14, when we have no other choice. In this case, tension is rewarded or 'reinforced' because it leads to a favorable outcome, namely escaping from a no-win scenario. However, many dilemmas are continuous with either option too important to ignore or avoid, and we possess faint hope of their resolution. That is often enough for us to dwell on such matters, even though the odds are long if not impossible. Sometimes these dilemmas represent future intractable issues, such as whether when traveling on vacation you worry, and are tense as you decide whether to turn back to see if you left the water on, and other times they represent a train of distractions from the internet to phone calls that provide moment to moment alternatives to doing one's work. And so we feel tense, and this pain or 'anxiety' forces our hand to make one decision or other, or else to simply escape the situation.

Muscles work to speed decision making, and that's often a good thing, lest we forget the lesson of Buridan's mule, who was indeed a real stupid ass. The question you may pose however is what makes you the author so sure? Simple, if perseveration on cognitive dilemmas is the cause of tension, and apart from fear, is the *only* cause of tension, then all the remedies for tension or stress must overtly or covertly rely on the remedy we propose. In the next chapter, we will demonstrate just that.

---

that have good and bad qualities, such as whether to order dessert after dinner. To have dessert means to indulge in a tasty treat and consume a lot of calories, in contrast to the alternative of rejecting the pleasure but avoiding resulting weight gain. Our own theory clearly defines the neuro-muscular component that causes the discomfort of anxiety, and explains anxiety by updating D and M's drive theory with modern concepts of incentive motivation that are rooted in actual neurological and physiological processes. Nonetheless, the essential element of both theories, that anxiety is reinforced by avoidance, is the same.

Chapter 3

Rest Unexplained

An astute reader will conclude that my proffered procedure for relaxation is hardly new, and is incorporated in one fashion or another in the myriad relaxation protocols that are available to us from meditation to simply lounging on the beach. And the reader would of course be correct. However, as I will demonstrate shortly, it is my *explanation* that is new, and it is explanation that informs the procedures you may derive, the observations you have made and will make, and allow us to focus on the true dynamics of behavior, and to throttle them back and forth at our convenience confident in our predicted results. Explanations are simply interlocking descriptions of events from a variety of complementary perspectives that in turn can range from the simple to complex that allow us to predict and control our world. Explanations are refutable, or in other words, subject to criticism. They are mutable conceptual objects that give us direction in life, and at our call, can be used to predict and control our worlds. To be scientific is to not simply describe, but to explain, and even for the most mundane aspects of life we need good explanations.

For example, for every ailment from a headache to the common cold, you treat the symptom and/or you treat the cause, and you know how to treat it because from the most complex to the simplest metaphorical sense, you can *explain* it. Consider an ear infection. Our explanations for infection can range from the very complex to the very simple. But whether you're a microbiologist or a school child, you nonetheless rely on simple explanations that like a rule of thumb guide you in your path. Anyone can explain what an infection is, and because of explanation we can be guided to the right remedy for its symptoms and its cure. We know that we can treat ear infections with antibiotics, pain relievers, bed rest, heat packs, or ear drops. All treat the symptoms, but only one remedy treats the cause. Because ear infections can be explained due to bacterial causes, we know therefore that antibiotics, or the body's natural immune response are the only cures. Thus, to cure an ear infection you take antibiotics or you rest in bed or simply wait, and allow your own immune system to fend it off. However, you will still of course likely address the symptoms, and ear drops, warm compresses, and pain relievers will help.

But let us consider a time when we did not have an explanation for ear infection. That's easy to do if we back up our analysis two hundred years are so. If you lived in 1815, and if you were forearmed with a correct explanation of infection, you would know that bed rest and the passage of time would be the only cure, awaiting our body's natural defenses to cure us. You would know that warm compresses and holding the head up to drain the middle ear would be effective therapies not to cure but to mitigate infection. Because you have an adequate explanation of infection, you can reject other remedies of the time that by want of mere correlation with a good result, or confounded with faulty explanations, were given credence they did not deserve. That means that prayers, exorcisms, and quack tonics are ruled out, and if you have some chicken soup, you would know its limitations.

Because you have a good explanation of what infections are and what they do, you can treat with and avoid infections, and know the difference between what treats the symptoms, what treats the cause, and what merely treats someone else's wallet. Your knowledge won't stop infections of course, but your ability to confront infection won't be stopped by bogus procedures that are informed only by tradition, old wives' tales, or dime store cures.

Above all, this little book attempts to provide a valid explanation of tension or stress. So how do we demonstrate this? A good explanation of course, but what does that mean? To have a good explanation, four criteria are necessary, simplicity, generality, testability, and justifiability.

A Good Explanation is Simple

Simple explanations are the coin of knowledge. They may be graduated to describe the same phenomena is greater detail, yet at root they can be understood as simple principles. We know for example that computer chips work with electricity and silicon and electronic gates, and that engines work through processes of internal combustion. We know also that organisms evolve, and that we get ill because of disease. These are simple explanations that we can easily ramp up to more complex explanations if we have the interest and the time. (And indeed the more complex iteration of my ideas is found in the appendix of this book) Yet simplicity remains key, for without it we are lost.

A Good Explanation has Generality

Explanations generalize to inform and improve current procedures, suggest new ones, and predict the failure of competing explanations and the procedures they entail. For example, understanding infection generalizes to many other diseases, and is a cornerstone to understand human biology and modern health. Similarly, Newtonian physics describes not just falling apples, but shooting cannons and shooting stars and orbiting moons. Like a tool set, generality allows us to do many things using just a simple set of principles, but doing is also predicting, and good explanations must therefore be primed to not just succeed, but also to fail.

A Good Explanation is Falsifiable

A good explanation's predictions are clear and general, and thus can be refuted easily. Moreover, they invite challenge so that they may be improved and strengthened, or else discarded. If your calculations demonstrate that a cannon ball will go so far given a certain mass and velocity, it will, and in all circumstances and all times. The same holds true for every widely held scientific explanation, from the theory of evolution to the theory of relativity. But if there is just one circumstance where the theory predicts a result that doesn't hold true, then the theory must be changed or even abandoned.

A Good Explanation Justifies

Ultimately, it may be said that people take aspirin not because it is a mysterious cure for a headache, but because it the *only* cure for a headache. Not knowing how aspirin works means that you will be receptive to other nostrums for your pain backed by false promises and spurious correlations, but knowing how aspirin works eliminates the need to consider alternatives and makes its acceptance universal. Inductive reasoning, or inferring causality from correlations, only multiplies competing correlations, and no one choice can be completely justified. The best exemplar of this is the uncertain justification of the practice of focal and mindfulness meditation. Although the procedures behind meditation 'work', the fact that they are not completely justified by an adequate explanation limits its universal acceptance as the primary cause for relaxation and 'happiness'.

Given these criteria for a good explanation, the question nonetheless remains, is our explanation indeed good? So far we have simply explained how muscular tension and relaxation occur, but does it work, and does it work in all circumstances that elicit tension? Our argument is that excepting circumstances where we are in fear, it does work, and has long been demonstrated to work. A key to the testability of our argument is the generality of our explanation. In other words, given the right perspective, has it been continually tested all along?

If cognitive perseveration is the primary reason behind the muscular tension that underlies our daily stress, then it logically follows that it is the core element behind our prescriptions for its relief. In other words, cognitive perseveration is the key to all instances of non-fear related stress, and is the core and often hidden principle for those procedures that are effective in reducing tension.

This is easily demonstrated through observation alone, gladly provided to us in the copious annals of the stress relief literature. However, procedures, no matter how effective, are no better than home tonics if they cannot be derived from explanation. In other words, to make a true chicken soup for the body or the soul, you need to know how chicken soup works. It's easy to come up with workable procedures or procedures which seem to work, and put off explanation for another time. For tension or 'stress' relief there seem to be hundreds of them, united in their glowing promises rather than explanations. So, let us examine how they are united or disunited by explanation.

Well-Tempered Procedures

Focal Meditation

Focal meditation is the sine qua non of procedures that induce relaxation, which means that it is the premier procedure to calm one's body and one's soul. Nonetheless, it remains a procedure without explanation, which of course has not stopped the growth in its popularity and the ever-growing expansiveness of its claims, from consciousness raising to increasing human virtue.

Focal meditation simply involves sharply reducing all thought in an undistracted environment. You are pretty much staring ahead and thinking of nothing, thus narrowing perceptions as well as eliminating decision making. As essentially 'thought less' awareness, meditation is the best and most proven way to relax. So, does that make it the best method? Well, no. In meditation, all perseverative choice is avoided, but so is *non-perseverative choice*. So, you avoid not just worry, rumination, and distraction, but any other decision making no matter how innocuous. You are not thinking about your troubles, but you aren't thinking about what to have for breakfast or the nature of the universe either. Thus, you become relaxed but are pretty useless to yourself and the world for the time being. As a method to achieve relaxation, meditation is thus effective, but not practical, since it is only performed in restrictive distraction free environments.

Mindfulness

Mindfulness may be described as 'choice less' or moment to moment awareness. It is a state of active, open attention on the present, but without the requirement to narrowing one's perceptual field or focal attention. However, mindfulness is like focal meditation because both avoid perseverative *and* non-perseverative decision making. Thus, both focal meditation and mindfulness are *over inclusive* of the cognitive events that need to be avoided to achieve rest. However, non-perseverative thought, and specifically thinking about choices that have meaning, stimulates or enhances attentive arousal or alertness, and eliminating it makes meditation ultimately boring, and therefore unsustainable. Because of this, both meditation and mindfulness represent cognitive operations that can only be performed periodically rather than continually, as our prescription for relaxation demands. Nonetheless, the elimination of perseverative thought alone may be construed to represent a *variant* of mindfulness, as it represents non-judgmental awareness of a subset of cognition, not all cognition.

Reducing perseverative cognition is a subset of meditative procedure, and eliminating non-perseverative cognition may be important as well, but for reasons other than reducing somatic arousal. This is specifically the case for our evolving knowledge of how the brain 'at rest' works. Salutary changes in brain chemistry and structure have been linked to a radical reduction in conscious decision making, but whether this is due to the lack of input from the musculature or a reduction in neural activity due to the reduction in decision making remains to be seen.[4]

---

[4] Perhaps the best way to understand mindfulness and how it presented to an admiring audience is to understand magic. Acts of magic involve performances that have no explanation, and our wonderment that they have none is a major part of their allure. To pull a rabbit out of a hat, once

Finally, it must be noted that although many studies that justify meditation duly contrast meditators with subjects who have undergone relaxation training, the relaxation training generally involves modifying the *symptomology* of tension through learning how to visualize and control the musculature (e.g., progressive relaxation techniques), not alter its cognitive cause, and is no more logical in proving the unique causality of meditation as an elicitor of rest than comparing the efficacy of an anti-histamine (which eliminates the symptoms) to an anti-viral (which eliminates the cause) for the treatment of a cold.

The Relaxation Response

Postulated by the cardiologist Herbert Benson, the 'relaxation response' is quite simple, and simply involves the rudiments of focal meditation, which is merely to sit in a quiet distraction free place and clear the mind of thoughts by reciting a simple precept or nonsense word. Aside from his dubious and unexplained position that the non-response of relaxation is in fact a response, cognitive perseveration is also avoided in such settings, and as with focal meditation, unnecessarily eliminates as well non-perseverative thought.

---

explained, is *old* hat, thus the magician wants to keep up the mystery, and surrounds the real and simple explanation (trap door connecting the hat to the bunny in the table) with a lot of gesticulating with magic words, hand gestures, and the waving of a magic wand. In a similar way, unexplained yet effective practices such as mindfulness have an aspect of magic. It helps that mindfulness has diverse meanings, so it can mean veritably anything. So if you are taking a time out from distraction, adding in superfluous procedural layers like deep breathing, intonations to be loving and kind, psychotherapeutic jargon, and four-day training seminars full of new age cant is easy to do for what amounts to a simple psychological hat trick.

Just Plain Rest

Lounging around and relaxing is the simplest way to rest, but is guided by the false notion that for rest, doing nothing is a proper substitute for thinking of nothing, or in the case of non-perseverative thought, thinking of something. Yet you can still relax while playing a game of chess, chopping wood, or pondering the nature of the universe and you can still be tense while in your moment of languor you are distracted by a nagging wife and needy children. For just plain rest, the elimination of perseverative thought is inadvertent, not planned. Thinking of nothing is simply the indirect result of doing nothing.

'Just plain rest' is not informed by explanation, and although it may also engage the reduction of perseverative thought, it may not do so with the consistency required to fully produce a relaxed state. Indeed, the superiority of meditative techniques to just resting is because they require a consistency in the reduction of perseverative thought, despite being bereft of explanation.

Better time management, improving skills, healthy diet, avoiding traffic, avoid arguments, positive thinking.

Improving your interpersonal and professional skills certainly ensures that there will be a lot less to worry about, but in comparison to generations past, we already *have* a lot less to worry about. That of course hasn't stopped a new age of security and abundance being labeled an 'age of anxiety'. The issue ultimately is not improving skill sets, but a continuing justification of a life full of worry and distraction. The issue ultimately is not practical, but as we will note in the final chapter of our book, philosophical.

Add more distraction

Novice sailors are warned that if they get thirsty, drinking sea water will assuage their thirst, but only for a short period, when the added salt compounds the thirst. Similarly, when we get bored or stressed at work, taking time out to access novel events such as social media, email, or simply chatting with a coworker reduces our tensions or ennui, but only for a time, and at the cost of creating another affective or distractive choice which conflicts with the rational utility of our present work. So, we remain stressed not only because of the conflicting choices reflective of the task at hand, but become *more* stressed because of distractive choices that are now an option.

Deep breathing, guided imagery, progressive relaxation, taking a herbal bath, stretching, getting a massage, rocking in a chair, counting sheep, taking a nap, or any other of the 540 or more ways to reduce stress.

Recipes for stress relief are like all recipes, the cure is the same but the secret is in the ingredients, which differ only in type, measure, application, and name. The permutations of such things make for stress remedies, and from a simple perusal of the stress relief literature, indeed they are. Stress tips are ubiquitous, and without them all the magazines on the checkout line of your local supermarket would be a lot thinner. Like diet and dating advice, stress remedies rarely differentiate between symptom and cure, and may only partially address the problem. Because stress tips don't derive from explanations, but mere experience, they cannot be judged against the metric *of* explanation. To relax means that you must *consistently* avoid *all* forms of perseverative thought from worry to distraction, not just treat the neuro-muscular symptoms of that thought. Comprehensiveness is key, you must touch all the bases, not a few. Besides lacking a good explanation, prevalent stress tips lack consistency. Thus, you can still suffer distractions or worry while walking on the beach or rocking on a chair, and to reduce the symptoms with a hot bath or massage does not eliminate the cause.

Profound Relaxation: Lessons from Meditation

A defining characteristic of meditative procedures is that they are practiced intermittently and over set periods of time. One practices meditation or mindfulness at certain hours during the day and for certain amounts of time, generally a half hour to an hour. The reduction of perseverative cognition through meditation gives the musculature the time to completely relax, and this state of persistent or profound relaxation elicits a state of pleasure or mild euphoria due to the concomitant and sustained elicitation of endogenous opioids (or endorphins) in the brain. The sustained increase of endogenous opioids also down regulates opioid receptors, and thus inhibits the salience or reward value of other substances (food, alcohol, drugs) that otherwise increase opioid levels, and therefore reduces cravings. Profound relaxation also mitigates our sensitivity to pain, and inhibits tension. In this way, relaxation causes pleasure, enhances self-control, counteracts and inhibits stress, reduces pain, and provides for a feeling of satisfaction and equanimity that is the hallmark of the so-called meditative state.

We normally do not associate relaxation with a natural high let alone deduce its benefits, and that is because we rarely have but a few minutes' respite from the next distractive event or thought. Because it is so unusual and unexpected, it is easy to ascribe a unique meditative state to meditative procedure, an inference that is easy to demonstrate as wrong. If perseverative cognition elicits tension, then the continuous avoidance of such cognition for an hour or so will result in total relaxation and a feeling of euphoria, along with greater self-control and rationality. Using a simple timer and charting your progress, anyone can demonstrate how profound relaxation is correlated to a few hours spent uninterrupted by distractive or other perseverative thought.

Despite the imputed generality of eliminating perseverative thought to achieve relaxation, the generality of our hypothesis must also apply to those situations that cause muscular tension, or stress. It is to that issue that we will now turn.

Chapter 4

A Matter of Stress

Stress is not just an academic concept, it is a daily and painful occurrence that impacts our personal productivity, happiness, and health, and understanding and treating it is a corresponding big business. Academic journals and the careers of countless psychologists have owed their existence to this emotion, and the sheer tonnage of commentary and study this emotion has wrought on the academic and popular imagination is extraordinary. Nonetheless, the causes of stress are quite simple, and can be rendered down to two simple themes.

Stress is due to Demand

*Stress is a problem when the **demands** on your time and energy go on all day, day after day, without letup-* **'Stress for Good' Book**

*The technical definition of stress is the amount of energy you need to adjust to the internal external **demands** of your life in a given amount of time. Stress is the balance between what you have to do and the resources you have to do it with.-* **Frederic Luskin**[1]

*Stress is a mediational process in which stressors (or **demands**) trigger an attempt at adaptation or resolution that results in individual distress if the organism is unsuccessful in satisfying demand.* - **W. Linden**[2]

*Stress is the non-specific response of the body to any **demand** made upon it.* - **Hans Selye**[3]

Stress is due to Threat

*Stress is a physical, mental and emotional response to a challenging event — not the event itself. Often referred to as the **fight-or-flight** response, the stress response occurs automatically when you feel threatened.* - **Mayo Clinic**

*Stress happens when we feel that we can't cope with pressure and this pressure comes in many shapes and forms, and triggers physiological responses. These changes are best described as the **fight or flight response**, a hard-wired reaction to perceived threats to our survival.* –**Stress Management Society.**

*This combination of reactions to stress is also known as the "**fight-or-flight**" **response** because it evolved as a survival mechanism, enabling people and other mammals to react quickly to life-threatening situations... Unfortunately, the body can also overreact to stressors that are not life-threatening, such as traffic jams, work pressure, and family difficulties.* - **Harvard Mental Health Letter**

*The stress response is also called the **fight-or-flight response**, as identified by Dr. Walter B. Cannon of the Harvard Medical School almost 100 years ago. The stress response is a profound set of involuntary physiological changes that occur whenever we are faced with a changing situation. The stress response, critical to the survival of primitive humankind, prepares the body for a physical reaction to a threat - to fight or flee.* - **Benson Henry Institute**

And again, stress may not have a proper definition at all!

.......there is no definition of stress that everyone agrees on, what is stressful for one person may be pleasurable or have little effect on others and we all react to stress differently. Stress is not a useful term for scientists because it is such a highly subjective phenomenon that it defies definition. -**American Institute of Stress**

So in light of these common definitions, the causes of stress should be simple. Get a little tense while on the job, therefore it's because you are suffering from a minor fear reaction, a tendency inherited from your caveman ancestors who had to fight or take flight when confronted with cave bears and tigers. On the other hand, it may simply be a matter of wear and tear, the inevitable result of inescapable workaday demand. The problem with such explanations is that they are not explanations at all, but are mere metaphors, and upon simple reflection and a little scientific knowledge bear no relationship to reality.

So, does demand cause stress? It seems reasonable to assume that the simple act of responding to the cognitive demands of the day causes some wear and tear on the body, leaving one exhausted from a hard day of mental work. But this belies the fact that many mentally demanding activities from climbing sheer cliffs to doing creative work correspond to a state of serene calm and emotional pleasure. Demanding activities such as work related pressure, coping with distractions, and worry about meeting a pending deadline do of course elicit tension, yet as a *type* of demand they differ from stress free demands because of choice conflicts, *not* choice content. In other words, a trivial demand such as fending off distraction is far more stressful than a major demand of creating a work of art or climbing a sheer cliff because the former represents choice conflict and the latter does not. So, does demand cause tension? Of course, but it is not *what* we are thinking about but *how* we are thinking about it that is the root cause of tension. So, then you may ask, if conflict free 'demand' does not cause stress, then what of the 'flight or fight' response that is so commonly attributed to stressful events?

It is a fact that our voluntarily and involuntary muscles are driven by our emotions, particularly when we are afraid or fearful. This 'flight or fight' response, or as it is known today as 'flight fight freezing system', or FFFS makes your heart race, your internal organs shut down, and primes your muscles to act to defend yourself, or else run for the hills. On the other hand, the simple tensions that occur when we find it hard to make up our minds activate the postural musculature alone, a simple response that shares little in common with the complex neurological and muscular reactions which comprise fear. In other words, see a spider far away and our postural muscles will move because we think, but see a spider on your nose, and all your muscles and a whole lot more will move because we fear. Do these separate instances correspond to the same neurological causes? Of course not. In both cases, you are avoiding the spider, and yet in each case your physiological responses are distinctively different not only in degree but also in kind.

Moreover, in the former case your behavior is driven because you think, and in the latter, it is because you are in fear. The former is due to cortical processes, and the latter is due to more primitive neural processes, centered in the midbrain, that govern the emotion of fear. This is a very simple distinction, verified conceptually as well as empirically (see appendix for academic sources), but it has not been explained well or has even been entertained in the copious academic and popular estimate of stress. So, our daily stresses and anxieties are distinctive from our fears. They are indeed *separate* emotions.

It is a remarkable fact that we've got stress figured out all wrong. Our hard-wired fear responses are responses to threat, not choice, and are governed by different neurological processes from those cortically based processes that underscore anxiety or tension. Secondly, neuromuscular tension due to choice conflict only activates the postural musculature, and the global changes in physiological activity, from a racing heart, hormonal changes, to enhanced alertness, vasodilation, hyperventilation, etc. simply are not characteristic of tension elicited by conflicted thought. Both muscular tension and relaxation are ultimately functions of the *relationship* rather than *content* of our choices. It would seem then that simply changing *how* we think than *what* we think of would be a snap, and that stress could be banished forever. That would indeed be the case if we were reasonable creatures, which as we will show in the next chapter, we are not.

Chapter 5

Affective Decisions

We begin our day, and likely all our days, unconcerned that a meteor will fall on our heads or that we will drop dead for any number of causes. It's simply a matter of just being there, since birth, with neither of these events happening to us, so far.

Now let us say that the grand prize in the Powerball lottery is now up to $500,000,000. Since the government has not enrolled us in the social perk of a mandatory daily enrollment in the lottery, we have never gained the experience of not winning. So, it is particularly novel that we now have the opportunity of winning a prize that has no more likelihood of coming our way than a meteor landing on our head. And so we buy Powerball tickets, and in spite of our knowledge of the impossible odds, keep our eyes and our pocketbooks open to new and unexpected possibilities that give new meaning to the phrase that our eyes are bigger than our stomachs.

The new un-likelihoods outshine the old un-likelihoods because that is how our brains proverbially shine, or should I say activate. For the purchaser of Powerball tickets, you can say he is literally of two minds regarding his choice. He knows that his odds are long and that the long term predicted value or 'utility' of buying a lottery ticket is next to nil. However, because the idea of winning the grand prize is unexpectedly novel or new, the immediate or 'decision' utility of buying the ticket is driven by a simple positive emotion, or positive affect. In other words, in the present moment a lottery ticket has value, but in the longer term it has none. For another example, consider a normal day at work. From moment to moment we can go about our necessary business, or take a moment to check our email, our social media page, chat with a coworker, or make an idle phone call. These behaviors have a predicted utility that diminishes to near zero the more often we do them within a space of time, but the momentary or 'decision' utility stays high because these behaviors are novel events with positive outcomes.

These examples demonstrate how the introduction of affect multiplies the dilemma of deciding between a bird in the hand and two in the bush to endless numbers of birds in endless numbers of bushes as far as the eye can see. The great majority of these choices have no future utility or value to us, yet we are torn between them nonetheless because one choice is affective and one choice is effective, choices that are hard if not impossible to reconcile.

So, what it the source of this positive effect? It is a brain chemical called dopamine, which is more formally regarded as a 'neuromodulator' which activates groups of brain cells to center attention and facilitate thinking, and is subjectively felt as a sense of energy, elation, or activation, but not ironically, pleasure. Dopamine is released upon the anticipation or experience of positive novel or discrepant events wherein moment to moment outcomes differ from what is expected. To be alert and aroused is a perquisite for living, and the feeling of boredom that occurs even when one is engaging in pleasurable activity (eating an ice cream cone, resting) reflects the actual pain that is present when dopamine levels are lowered due to a lack of novel or 'meaningful' activity. Dopamine activity is further depressed with the perception of events that have *negative* meaning, such as the imminent prospect of death and taxes, and the resulting and painful state of depression results in a loss of ability to focus attention and to think clearly. A primary role for dopamine is to change the importance or salience of moment to moment behavior. This momentary salience may or may not conform to the overall importance of an extended behavior sequence, but it does not and cannot *predict* the long-term importance of that sequence. For example, intermittent small wins on a slot machine increase the salience or moment to moment importance of each pull of the lever, and the decision utility of the moment may or may not conform to a winning jackpot, but it nonetheless cannot predict whether in the long run a jackpot will occur. Dopamine only influences the value of the here and now, but besides often setting us off in eccentric and wrongheaded directions, it makes cognitive perseveration not just optional, but almost guaranteed.[5]

In other words, we are literally of 'two minds' in many decisions, and that often entails cognitive dilemmas that would have been resolved in a second if affect had not skewed our thinking. So, we are susceptible to perseverative conflicts between nearby 'bright and shiny objects' and the duller path of rational thinking and rational goals.

So, what's a thinking person to do?

As we will argue, there is a tried and true solution that is millennia old, and is no less than a philosophical whack on the head.[6]

---

[5] And it may be argued, dopamine may be behind not just our distractions, but also our worries. For example, we may logically regard as extremely unlikely the likelihood that we have left our house unlocked as we embark on a trip, yet like the Powerball example, the affective value of that likelihood may skew our thinking, and have us running back to check on our house in what in foresight and hindsight is clearly an irrational behavior.

[6] (And here is a more formal explanation of how affective choice relates to stress, based on the work of the neuropsychologist **Kent Berridge**.)

Our mammalian ancestors were motivated by events that had survival value, and these events were ingrained as the necessary pleasures of existence, such as food, sex, and drink. However, their world, as is ours, was uncertain, and evolution required an additional inborn 'instinct' to persistently drive an animal to convert the uncertain into the certain, the unknown into the known. This seeking or foraging instinct gave utility or value to moment to moment exploratory behavior. The foraging instinct is embodied in a state of arousal (rendered by mid brain dopamine systems) that incents an animal to render from uncertainty the safe and sure paths to the hedonic outcomes (rendered by mid brain opioid systems) of food, drink, and potential mates, and to indirectly insure that pleasures are not only assured for now, but in the days and weeks to come. For foraging animals, the utility of the present moment or *decision utility* generally conforms to the future or *predicted utility* of hedonic outcomes. When the animal is not foraging, it rests, which is also hedonic in nature due to similar opioid responsiveness to relaxed states. So, for foraging animals in uncertain environments, their motivation is sustained by interdependent or synergistic affective states or 'utilities' that are maintained by different neurological systems.

For human beings, a widely help premise in philosophy is that the purpose of life is to maximize experienced 'utility', or pleasure. Pleasurable events are predicated in the future (food, sex, shelter) and in the present (neuro-muscular deactivation or rest). Both are defined through the activation of opioid systems in the brain. But like our foraging ancestors, our day to day goals also embody a degree of moment to moment uncertainty that also activates dopamine systems that see us through our daily affairs. Unfortunately, whereas nature aligns decision utility with experienced utility, so that for animals foraging behavior is rarely in vain, such is not the case with human beings, who can create decision utility which is untethered to productive or valuable outcomes.

Decision utility that contrasts with predicted utility elicits an 'approach-approach' conflict between different values instantiated by different neurological causes that cannot be reconciled. Such 'distractive' events are correlated with neuromuscular activation that if sustained causes pain and that also eliminates the experienced utility or pleasure of relaxation. Decision utility is generally desirable only if it conforms to experienced utility, as it enables us to focus on obtaining pleasurable outcomes and sustain present pleasurable ones (relaxation). Animals in the wild are in general not stressed because nature aligns the utilities that guide their behavior. For human beings, this alignment is easily broken because of higher order processes of thought that maximize decision utility, but often misalign it with non-productive behavior. This is characterized in a modern world that is full of novel events that are important when they align with our productivity, yet are pernicious (as distraction) when they do not. It is up to *explanation* and informed individual choice, not government fiat, which permits us to sort them out.

Our freedom of choice is constrained by our explanations of how the world works. When our explanations are wrong, as they were in ancient and even recent times, then we are condemned to the medieval barbarism of pain and suffering. If the explanations are correct, then we can make the right choices that guarantee our pleasures, well-being, and human dignity. A proper definition of stress, based upon neurologically grounded principles of incentive motivation, is the first step in making this happen.

Chapter 6

A not so new Rationalism

"There is only one way to happiness and that is to cease worrying about things which are beyond the power of our will." – Epictetus (ca. 115AD)

"Don't worry, be happy"- Bobby McFerrin (ca. 1988AD)

Times were tough all over. Thousands of illegal aliens were crossing the border, the economy was in decline, people spent their days in mindless and generally violent entertainment, the Middle East was in chaos, the environment was degraded and the prophets all agreed, the end of world was near. Our civilization will follow that of the Roman Empire, unless you are of course living during the Roman Empire, and then you've really got troubles!

So, let's go back two thousand years to the year 115. The Roman Empire was at its height, government was bureaucratic yet just, bread and circuses were free, and naturally, folks were miserable. It was the time of the Pax Romana, or Roman peace, but that didn't stop people, then as now, from complaining about the macro and micro aggressions that made miserable their days.

With a nascent Christianity and other oriental religions, the consolation of theology was that evil will get its due, that the meek will inherit the earth, there was a heavenly reward for putting up with all your suffering, and it pays to be loving and kind, even if you get shafted in the end.

So, what was the competing consolation of philosophy at the time? Enter the philosophy of Stoicism. The Stoics were pragmatic philosophers who looked to real world results. Their 'consolation' was no promise of heaven or divine intervention, but rather a philosophical whack on the head. Things may be hopeless, but that does not mean you should be hapless, and it was haplessness that was the true cause of our misery. Their primary advice was simple, stop worrying and fretting about things you have no control over! In other words, it is sheer delusion to consider worry and rumination as coping strategies because they will not get you any closer to resolving your problems. Cognitive perseveration is a waste of time and energy, and you should focus the things that you have control over, namely your own character, integrity, and personal virtue. Only then can you be truly happy, and happiness is a personal choice derived from reason, not a gift from the gods.

The Stoic ideal was frankly Greek rather than Christian in nature, but they were no slouches in ethics. Indeed, to them it was all that cognitive perseveration on hopeless choices and causes that make people into unhappy crude and brutish sorts. Eliminate all that consternation between decisions you have no control over, and you will end up being the reasonable and relaxed sort that is after all your true nature anyways, and your personal character and confidence will gain from it to boot.

What the Stoics didn't have of course was an explanation as to why clear thinking was the one true road to emotional health and happiness. Because they couldn't explain their philosophy, they could not justify it, and Stoic teachings became relegated mainly to Bartlett's familiar quotations. But with explanation, the Stoic ideal becomes not just practical, but wholly justified, and it is to our not so original procedure that in full circle we return.

Chapter 7

Parsing Happiness

How do you make a lion, a tiger, or a bear happy?

Simply put, you just meet their needs. Give them food, drink, a proper mate, and they will be happy.

Well, almost. They also need the ability to roam freely in an uncertain environment. If not, as zoo keepers would attest, the best cared for animal would quite literally go mad.

Animals know their needs are met because they can *feel* them being met, and feelings are *affective* states that are mediated by specific neurochemicals in the brain. The pleasures of life, from food to rest, are mediated by opioid systems, whereas a feeling of alertness or arousal (but not pleasure) is mediated by dopamine systems that are activated by the experience or anticipation of novel or unexpected events that have positive outcomes[4]. Opioids also have an excitatory effect on dopamine systems and vice versa.[5,6,7] Thus, not only do opioids increase dopamine levels; but opioid activity is potentiated due to dopamine activation. Therefore, to maximize arousal and pleasure, both need to be accentuated. In other words, opioid and dopamine systems are *synergistic*, or their combined effects are greater than the sum of their separate effects. Maximize both concurrently, and in the case of animals at least, you will have a very happy critter.

For human critters, we are distinctively different from animals in large measure because of a large neo-cortex that allows us to virtually render behavior and its myriad uncertain outcomes. In other words, we can mentally rehearse or think through options prior to choosing them, thus giving them meaning, and activate the same dopamine systems. We will define 'meaning' as the branching positive and novel implications of behavior as perceived *virtually*. For example, recreating the super bowl on a video console has little meaning, but watching the real super bowl does, and doing a good deed, earning a degree, or completing a work of art bestows a sense or 'feeling' of honor, pride, or achievement that represent ever refreshing meaning. We want to consider past and present behavior and the emblems of that behavior (trophies, rewards) to have meaningful cognitive import that branch into endless positive and affective implications, that will in other words 'echo into eternity'. When combined with the pleasurable affective state of rest, a maximal state of pleasure and alert arousal will be achieved.

The subtle but major flaw in most resting procedures (e.g. meditation) is that they eschew meaning, and diminish or dismiss the alert arousal that humans instinctively require to live productive lives and escape the pangs of boredom.[7] Conversely, a life of meaning but full of meaningful but irresolvable conflicts eliminates the pleasurable state of relaxation and replaces it with the pain of tension or 'stress'. Contemporary philosophies of life commonly separate the two, as if pleasure and purpose are entirely separate and often conflicting goals. Quite the opposite, they are interdependent.

---

[7] And a subtle but major flaw in meditation *research* is that it does not address the *affective* component of meditative states, which clearly implicate relaxation and states of alert arousal and the perceptual events which elicit them. Meditation research generally relies upon comparative self-reports of meditators and non-meditators, or fmri (functional magnetic resonance imaging) or brain scans that measure cerebral blood flow. However, neither can isolate the neuro-muscular and neuro-chemical activity that correlate with subjective affective states, or how neuro-muscular activity is a function of cortical activity as mapped to experience or learning. Because these research methods and tools cannot determine the etiology or source of the positive affect associated with meditation, it is no surprise that meditation remains without an adequate explanation.

The Affective Bootstrap

The necessity of a life of pleasure *and* attentive arousal (or meaning) ultimately dovetails to our prescription in the preface of our book, and argues that separate affective systems in the brain can effectively 'bootstrap' each other if each is concurrently activated through simple cognitive means. Thus, set aside a large and continuous amount of your time for meaningful behavior and/or thinking of future behavior that has meaning, and concurrently avoid the meaningful conflicts or perseverative cognitions that induce tension, and you will be alert, aroused, and pleasurably relaxed. You will maximize positive affect in both its major forms, and you will be happy. Ultimately, if happiness is defined affectively, then to be positively affective, one must be *effective*. A life of meaning, bereft of distraction and other perseverative thought, is the key to happiness. It is that simple, and is as simply attained.[8]

---

[8] The study of the affective concomitants of a meaningful and focused engagement with the world is not new, and finds it best contemporary advocate in the work of the humanistic psychologist Mihaly Csikszentmihalyi, who coined the term 'flow experience' to reflect self-reports of artists, athletes, and other individuals who uniformly reported a very intense and positive affective state when engaged in tasks that had very high and consistent meaning that engaged their undistracted attention. The twain meets of course when our 'bottoms up' approach to affect interlocks with Dr. C's 'top down' perspective, which although highly metaphorical in nature, nonetheless conforms to neurological truths. A much more detailed analysis of the flow experience is found on pages 71-74 of this book.

Appendix

Now it's time for a more complex explanation. You know the sort, full of new words, inscrutable argument, and a list of referential sources whose validity you must take on the author's word but whose simple implications should be subject to challenge and refutation. In this section I will wade into the fine print of a higher order explanation for muscular tension and relaxation. For those wanting to delve into even the finer print of my analysis I refer you two articles by this author that have long since disappeared into the Sargasso Sea of academic literature. The latter of these two articles appeared in 2010 in the Journal 'The Behavior Analyst Today', and was the companion piece of an earlier article published in 2006 in the 'International Journal of Stress Management' (links provided).

https://www.scribd.com/doc/16384355/Stress-and-the-Cinderella-Effect

https://www.scribd.com/doc/121345732/Relaxation-and-Muscular-Tension-A-bio-behavioristic-explanation

The following argument restates more formally our position, and discusses the larger implications of an explanation of muscular relaxation and tension in the context of popular theories and schematics of emotion, which include the Yerkes-Dodson law, 'Circumplex' theories of emotion, and the concept of 'flow'.

The Rest of 'Rest'

Muscle Bound

Almost forty percent of our body weight is our muscles, comprising skeletal, cardiac, and abdominal groups, and skeletal muscles alone are over 620 in number. Naturally, understanding how these muscles work, grow, tire, and are repaired is important not only for health and fitness, but also in terms of how we move about and handle our world. Understanding how they work is also, as we have argued in our little book, about motivation.

For the striated or voluntary musculature, motivation is easy. Grasping, walking, talking, etc. occur or are 'emitted' because they are followed by or are 'reinforced' by specific discrete outcomes. We act in other words because actions do things. Because these behaviors uniformly engage a specific organelle of the body, namely the striated musculature, a common presumption is that this 'operant' conditioning primarily reflects the activity of these muscles. Of course, convulsions, fear reactions, startle reactions, etc. *do* involve the striated musculature and can be mediated by neurological rather than purely cognitive causes, but in general muscular activity is guided by its functionality as consciously perceived.

It is commonly assumed that if striated muscles are activated, they may be observed by everyone, and thus everyone can see and agree to the obvious fact that they are universally correlated with getting things done, and are thus operant behaviors. Yet only a fraction of striated muscular activity is observable by anyone or even yourself. That is, the musculature may be activated yet not result in publicly observable responses, and neither may it be consciously or privately perceived by the individual. Ironically, the non-conscious activity of the musculature has long been made public through devices such as the skin conductance response (SCR) and electromyography (EMG), but rarely if ever has this behavior been hypothesized to respond to non-consciously perceived outcomes. Rather, muscular tension has generally been construed to be an artifact of autonomic arousal that is elicited due to psycho-social 'demand'. This interpretation regards muscular tension as controlled by different motivational principles from those that underscore voluntary or operant behavior, such as the reflexive or stimulus-response reactions entailed by a fight or flight response, stress reaction, etc.[8] In this case, inferred instinctive processes take the place of observed cause and effect relationships between behavior and outcomes.

However, this conclusion may remain uncontested not because the relationship between tension and a change in overt behavior is disproven, or because the relevant data are unobtainable, but because of a common misinterpretation of the meaning of 'demand'. But before we delve into semantics of how we understand motivation, we must first understand how striatal muscles work.

The Striated Musculature

Although the activity of the striated musculature comprises most behavior as we understand it, its psychophysiology is not widely known. Muscle fibers are categorized into "slow-twitch fibers" and "fast-twitch fibers."[9] Slow-twitch fibers (also called "Type 1 muscle fibers") activate and deactivate slowly, but when activated they are also very slow to fatigue. Fast-twitch fibers activate and deactivate rapidly and come in two types: "Type 2A muscle fibers" which fatigue at an intermediate rate, and "Type 2B muscle fibers" which fatigue rapidly. These three muscle fiber types (Types 1, 2A, and 2B) are contained in all muscles in varying amounts. Muscles that need to be activated much of the time (like postural muscles) have a greater number of Type 1 (slow) fibers. When a muscle starts to contract, primarily Type 1 fibers are activated first, followed by Type 2A, then 2B. Type 1 fibers are often continuously activated because of psychosocial 'demand' that in general does not engage fast twitch fibers. For an individual, this activation is only indirectly observed when these fibers subsequently fatigue, causing exhaustion and pain.

Muscular activation also causes major changes in the autonomic nervous system. Sympathetic autonomic arousal is elicited through the sustained contraction of high threshold motor units (Type 2) of the striated musculature, as occurs during running or weight training.[10] But arousal may also be mediated by the sustained contraction of small low threshold motor (Type 1) units of the striated musculature,[11] and can be measured directly through EMG (electromyogram) or through indirect measures of autonomic arousal (e.g., skin conductance response or SCR; galvanic skin response or GSR) elicited by tension induced arousal. Physiologically, the neural pathways that detail how muscular tension instigates autonomic arousal have been well established. [12] [13] [14] [15] Through a bi-directional connection between the reticular arousal system and muscle efferents, a dramatic decrease or increase in muscle activity throughout the body can respectively stimulate decreases or increases in sympathetic arousal. Critical to the reduction of sympathetic arousal is the elicitation of endogenous opioids through neuro-muscular inactivity that not only diminishes stress-induced neuroendocrine and autonomic responses, but also stimulate these effector systems in the non-stressed state.[16] In addition, chronic or sustained opioid activity down regulates opioid receptors, thus reducing the palatability of and craving for other substances (e.g. food or alcohol).[17] In other words, relaxation or resting not only counteracts the deleterious effects of sympathetic arousal, but is subjectively experienced as a state of mild euphoria or pleasure due to the concomitant activity of opioid systems.(1)

This striated muscle position hypothesis[18] holds that the critical controlling event for autonomic arousal is covert neuro-muscular activity, and that rapid striated muscular activity can "mediate and thereby control what has been called autonomic, cardiovascular, and electroencephalographic conditioning." The question yet unanswered is how covert muscular activity is conditioned.

Contingency and Demand

The contraction of Type 1 fibers occurs prior to and in tandem with type 2 muscular activation, and is essential to voluntary behavior. Type 1 activation also occurs to prime an individual for action and as such is also dependent upon the anticipated results of that activity. It thus follows that Type 1 fibres are commonly activated due to due to perceived causes and effects or 'response contingencies'. However, if type 1 muscular contraction occurs without the subsequent activation of type 2 musculature, then involuntary or reflexive mechanisms are generally inferred to occur by the 'stimulus' of demand. For example, a worker who 'multi-tasks' between several tasks and is subject to the distractions of co-workers, email, etc., normally attributes sustained tension and emotional exhaustion to the 'demands' of working day. The metaphor of demand connotes a stimulus event that *elicits* tension rather than contrasting response contingencies that cause tension to be *emitted*. But does this concept of demand denote a true mechanism or is it merely a misrepresentation of the semantics or meaning of demand?

1. Neuro-muscular activity in the form of light aerobic activity (walking, stretching, doing housework) has also been hypothesized to increase endogenous opioids or endorphins (e.g. yoga), but only strenuous aerobic activity (e.g. long distance running) has been demonstrated to induce the production of endorphins.[19] However, endorphin production is reflected in blood levels, and not in the brain. Endorphins in the blood cannot pass the blood-brain barrier, but the neurotransmitter called anandamide can, which is elevated after strenuous exercise and *can* travel from the blood to the brain. Anandamide is as an endocannabinoid, similar to the psycho-activating element of marijuana, and it is also accompanied by the increase in serotonin or norepinephrine levels that in lower levels are correlated with depression. It is they and not endogenous opioids that likely constitute the 'runners high'.[20]

As popularly conceived, tension is a result of reflexive processes (e.g. flight or fight) that are elicited by a requirement for performance represented by 'threat' or 'demand'. But the requirement for performance entails a conscious or non-conscious appraisal of the consequences dependent *upon* performance or non-performance and the variability or likelihood of those outcomes. These represent future contingent outcomes. Thus, demand *must* implicate cause and effect, or contingency. Demand also entails the conscious or non-conscious appraisal of different response options or contingencies that lead to a similar end. Furthermore, demand occurs in a perceptual space that involves the concurrent consideration of alternative response contingencies that lead to dissimilar ends (e.g. distractions). In other words, *demand entails choice*. For example, a person confronting a demand to complete a project at work must choose between different response options (e.g. work faster, take short cuts), and his performance is further influenced by the availability of alternative response options (e.g. taking a break). Hence demand cannot represent a stimulus event that elicits behavior, but rather denotes alternative response contingencies or choices that lead to the emission *of* behavior.

Besides the cognitive element of demand, tension and associated arousal are also correlated with cognitive events that represent abstract rather than normative (i.e. means-end) properties of a contingency. It has been proposed that discrepant, unpredicted, or novel events directly elicit alarm or arousal states.[21] A variant of this hypothesis proposes that discrepant events first elicit affective events which *in turn* "automatically and obligatorily elicit a somatic response." [22] [23] [24] In short, the "primary inducer is a stimulus in the environment (i.e. risk) that elicits an emotional response."[25] For example, a person winning the lottery or who suddenly learns he owes money on his income tax perceives novel rewarding or aversive outcomes, and feels tense because of the unexpectedness or novelty of the event or because of the affective events elicited by those outcomes. Nonetheless, the reflexive or 'automatic' link between somatic (i.e. sympathetic) arousal and unpredictable, discrepant, or risky events is not supported by the facts. Indeed, continuous positive surprise or discrepancy[26] as evidenced in creative and sporting behavior is highly correlated with profound relaxation and low autonomic arousal. For example, a rock climber involved in the 'touch and go' behavior of climbing a difficult cliff experiences low autonomic arousal or is 'cool under pressure' when his moment to moment risky behavior is successfully accomplished. Similarly, an artist in the thrall of a creative act feels elated but relaxed during the moment to moment novelty of inspiration. Finally, low autonomic arousal is characteristic when avoidance from surprising painful events (e.g. bad news) is impossible, as in the case of 'learned helplessness'.[27] Thus we may feel depressed and non-anxious when we learn of bad news wherein there is no recourse, such as a fatal illness, natural disaster, etc. As an alternative explanation, because affective events intrinsically change the value of the behavior that accompanies them, this behavior may also contrast with other alternatives that have value derived from a cognitive or rational domain. In other words, emotional value alters the relative value of alternative choices, and hence may signal the emission of covert somatic (i.e. neuro-muscular) behavior. Thus, it is proposed that *discrepancy elicited affect does not directly elicit sympathetic arousal, but can indirectly establish a contrast between response alternatives that does.*

These concepts are easily illustrated through the facts of behavior. Specifically, sustained or 'tonic' levels of muscular tension are commonly produced under continuous or moment to moment alternative choices wherein any choice entails near equivalent feasible or avoidable losses, or dilemmas. These dilemmas may consist of two or more rationally comparable choices that are near equivalent (e.g. what choice to make in a card game) or two choices that represent affective choices or affective vs. rational choices that are near equivalent in value and cannot be logically compared.[28] An affective choice will be defined as an anticipatory emotion or more specifically, a priming effect due to the enhanced and sustained activity of mid-brain dopamine systems[29] that provide an affective value (or 'wanting') to engaging in or the prospect of engaging in positive unpredicted or novel events (e.g. checking email) or primary drives (e.g. 'wanting' an ice cream cone). *(2)* As such this activity may occur not only when a discrepancy is perceived (as represented by the primary inducer), but also from moment to moment *prior* to or in anticipation of that event (as represented by the secondary inducer). Thus, continuous decision making between alternative choices (e.g. doing housework or minding a child, working or surfing the internet, staying on a diet or eating ice cream, keeping a dental appointment or staying at home) represents irreconcilable affective and/or rational alternatives wherein one choice entails the loss of its

alternative, and is associated with sustained or tonic levels of tension that is painful. Called the 'Cinderella Effect' from the fairy tale character who as a harried servant girl was first to wake and last to sleep, [30] [31] [32] [33] the continuous activation of type 1 motor units or muscles (also called Cinderella fibers) because of this psycho-social 'demand' causes them to eventually fail, and thus recruit other groups of muscles more peripheral to the original group, resulting in pain and exhaustion. In addition, as the name Cinderella suggests, these slow twitch fibers are slow to deactivate, and will continue activated even during subsequent intervals of rest.[34] The aversive result of this long-term activation conforms to McEwen's model of 'allostatic load',[35] which predicts that tension and

2. The neuro-modulator dopamine is implicated in all learning, and is released upon the anticipation or experience of novel or discrepant events wherein moment to moment outcomes differ from what is expected. Dopamine release increases with the importance or salience of an event,[36] and is felt as a sense of energy, pleasure, or activation. Thus, one feels more energized or elated upon winning the lottery if the prize is large rather than small. A major role for dopamine is to change the importance or 'incentive salience' of moment to moment behavior.[37] This momentary salience may or may not correspond to the overall importance of an extended behavior sequence. For example, intermittent small wins on a slot machine increase the salience or moment to moment importance of gambling even though the

long-term consequences (namely a large cumulative loss) is the inevitable consequence.

arousal will be maladaptive when there is an imbalance between activation and rest/recovery. Specifically, continuous low level or 'slight' tension results in overexposure to stress hormones, high blood pressure, and resulting mental and physical exhaustion. It must be remarked that in these examples slight tension is correlated with moment to moment choices between alternatives that have *low* salience, and is characteristic of common day to day choices. However, if the choice salience was very high, wherein alternative choices represent highly salient possible outcomes such as matters of life and death, then tension and arousal would be much higher, and would be reported as anxiety.[38]

It must be noted that anxiety is a separate emotion from fear, or the flight or fight response. The flight/fight fleeing system (FFFS) is activated by situations that entail imminent threat. In the popular literature of stress, the FFFS is commonly invoked for autonomic arousal occurring across all threatening and non-threatening situations. However, for distant threats (e.g. a spider approaching from a great distance away as compared to a spider an inch from your nose), or for non-threatening choice/choice conflicts (e.g., distractive conflicts), the FFFS is not activated. Thus, covert neuro-muscular activity in these situations cannot be attributed to instinctive flight/fight neural mechanisms, but to cortical activity,[39] therefore implicating learning processes.

Finally, in addition to continuous choices, intermittent choices between conflicting near equivalent low salience response options also correlate with tension induced arousal, and this activity is correspondingly intermittent or 'phasic'. Because tension is quickly followed by a period of rest and recovery, tension is still affective and painful, but it is not maladaptive.

Overall, whether continuous or intermittent, the demand reflected by near equivalent choices does not represent a discrete stimulus or stimuli that bypass cognition but rather comprises a cognitive event that denotes changing perceptual relationships between behavior and outcomes. These alternative choices describe responses that lead to primary gains at the cost of moment to moment opportunity losses. Thus the primary gain of doing one's work or accessing the internet comes at the moment to moment opportunity loss of the novel event of accessing social media, events that are not reconcilable logically since the former represents an effective or instrumental event and the latter an emotional or affective one. But what is the purpose of concurrent muscular activation? The sustained activation of type 1 fibers as elicited by the perception of equivalent alternative choices serves no direct functional purpose, but it may serve an indirect one. Sustained tension is painful, and as a rule pain imposes a new action priority to escape pain and to avoid future pain.[40] That is, pain serves to initiate avoidance behavior. In other words, pain is something you wish to escape. Thus, the pain of tension may serve to motivate an individual to escape from 'no win' situations when confronted with choices that entail significant gains but also significant loss, and tension is thus indirectly reinforced by the avoidance of the situation. (3) But if tension is due to information about the consequences of behavior, namely the avoidance of the painful results of tension, how can this be demonstrated?

3. A 'no win' situation predicts significant gains as well as significant opportunity losses if an individual continues to perform under alternative choices. These anticipated negative changes are painful,[41] and the awareness of future pain may signal muscular tension and corresponding avoidance behavior.[42] [43] A 'no win' situation may be also defined as an 'approach-avoidance' conflict, wherein we are simultaneously attracted and repelled by a goal that represents both an opportunity gain and opportunity loss. This conforms to the Dollard and Miller theory of anxiety[44] that argues that sympathetic autonomic arousal or 'anxiety' is elicited by a choice conflict, and is reinforced by the avoidance of the choice situation.

Resting Procedures

The argument for the operant nature of type 1 muscular activity is that if tension only occurs when decisions result in moment to moment or imminent feasible or avoidable (i.e., opportunity) losses due to near equivalent choices, then tension will *not* occur if there is no possibility of avoidance of future events, or no opportunity loss. That is, the loss remains, but the opportunity to avoid it does not. Thus, if tension occurs because it signals behavior that leads to the subsequent avoidance of the events that elicit tension, then it logically follows that tension is therefore 'reinforced' *by* prospective avoidance, and is an operant behavior.

A well-known procedure used to eliminate the ability to avoid loss while responding under multiple alternative choices is called an exclusion time out[45]. Common in educational environments, an exclusion time out describes a period when an individual is restrained from performing *all* actions which are otherwise rewarding to extinguish targeted behavior (e.g. temper tantrums). Thus, a child under time out must sit and not participate with classmates, engage in learning tasks, read a book, etc. Although the child incurs and is aware of loss, the difference is that this loss is unavoidable or non-feasible. A time out is also a resting procedure. To rest is to take a time out from the choices or demands of a working day to achieve a state of relaxation. However, it does not implicate to what degree choices are reduced, mainly that they are. Thus, although resting may figuratively represent an exclusion time out, it does not literally match the definition. To do that requires a *radical reduction of choices that entail imminent (i.e., moment to moment) feasible or opportunity loss*, and this is implicitly or explicitly entailed in meditative procedures. The research consensus is that meditative procedures and resting protocols correlate with an attendant state of relaxation.[46] [47] For meditation and resting, an individual may be aware of or is 'mindful' of irreconcilable choices due to rumination, worry, or distraction, but by not dwelling or perseverating on them, tension is eliminated by the avoidance of choice.

However, although the result of relaxation is shared by meditative and resting states, the inferred causes for these have been expanded beyond the mere reduction of choice. Thus, for meditation, relaxation may not be primarily attributed to the reduction of choice, but to the manipulation of attention. This manipulation involves focusing attention on a stimulus event (focal meditation, Benson's 'relaxation response'). But as with the meaning of demand, the meaning of focused attention is also ill defined, and must also entail the restriction of choice. In effect, the focusing of attention restricts choice by avoiding environmental events or the perception of the consequences of those events, which conforms to the definition of mindfulness as choice-less awareness.[48] Because meditation *must* entail moment to moment choice-less awareness or mindfulness, it may be inferred that the primary effect of meditation, namely muscular relaxation, is also due to the mindful or choice-less awareness implicit in meditation.

To reinterpret meditative and resting protocols as a 'time out' or 'choice-less awareness' makes the causes for relaxation equivalent. Thus, meditation *is* rest because their respective results *and* causes are the same. Because type 1 musculature is easily activated and is slow to deactivate, nearly all choice that entails moment to moment imminent feasible loss due to conflicting choices must be eliminated or deferred for a continuous period for the musculature to totally relax, and this is what meditative and resting protocols implicitly do, and for mindfulness procedures, it is what they *explicitly* do. Yet because muscular activation is not painful or harmful unless it is sustained, it is the *persistence* and not the degree of muscular activation that is deleterious. Thus, rumination and worry cause tension through the continuous or perseverative cognitive representation of near equivalent or incommensurate past or future choices. In addition, in this modern age, perseverative decision making between present choices or distraction is much more common, often continuous and inescapable, and results in the persistent activation of the musculature. Specifically, we consciously populate our environment with continuous distractive choices from email to the web, but continue to misattribute the resulting tension to the content rather than *context* of our choices. That is, by emphasizing what choices we make rather than how our choices are related to each other, the origin of muscular tension derives from the wrong cause and engenders the wrong 'cure'. Thus, choice becomes incidental to tension as the latter is attributed to the level of activity rather than the choices engendered *by* that activity. The remedy for this error entails ultimately a redefinition of the very concept of stress itself.

The Meaning of Stress

"If you wish to converse with me, define your terms" (Voltaire).

In his class, the psychologist F. J. McGuigan[49] would induce relaxation in his students through the technique of progressive relaxation. He would then drop a book to demonstrate how the startle reflex and associated arousal is inhibited or impossible without the presence of muscular tension, a finding originally made by Sherrington[50] and explained neurologically by Gellhorn.[51] This underscored the physiological fact that tension is primarily not the result of arousal, but its cause. If the independent measure of choice is added to the equation, the theoretical principle follows that *tension is the body's specific response to near equivalent alternative choices*. Because it indirectly controls and is controlled by the prospect of the occurrence or nonoccurrence of future events or reinforcers, tension indirectly acts on the environment or is an operant behavior. However, although tension and accompanying sympathetic arousal may be characterized as stress, it cannot be formally defined as stress. This is because the latter's terms are not precisely defined.

An operant definition of tension differs from Selye's classic definition of stress as "the body's nonspecific response to a demand placed on it."[52]

Yet these two principles are incompatible not because of their predictions but because of their meaning or *semantics*. That is, Selye's principle is not a scientific hypothesis because its terms are not clearly defined.

Ultimately, tension is initiated by the perception of means end response contingencies or expectancies due to the perseveration or dwelling on irreconcilable choices between past (rumination), present (distraction) or future (worry) events. Tension is in turn causes pain, which in turn intrinsically denotes the avoidance behaviors that will remove the tension that causes it. This is particularly important in the analysis of stress, since the common representation of stress implies that stress is a 'reaction' to demand events that bypass appraisal or cause and effect. However, whether tension and arousal are stress or represent a kind of stress is immaterial to the pragmatic implications of an operant analysis of tension. Specifically, if the metaphor of 'choice' replaces the metaphor of 'demand' as the primary descriptor of the origin of tension, then how choices are arranged may provide a much more precise and uniform description of the operational measures that will permit us to predict and control the daily tensions that beset us. Nonetheless, this argument is won not by the simplicity and precision of a learning based explanation, but through the power of procedure to effect behavioral change. That of course is the mandate and justification of psychology.

The Wheel of Emotion

Life in the Abstract

If you want to navigate your world, it is helpful to start with four dimensions rather than two. Three physical dimensions plus the dimension of time are enough to plot when and where you are, but to predict where you are going; the basic motivational dimensions are just as simple. You start with goals that have a future or predicted utility, correct from moment to moment your estimate of your progress and that of the goal itself, and correct your estimate of the feasible contrasting behavior and goals that you could have chosen. In other words, from moment to moment you are making choices both consciously and non-consciously between different exclusive alternatives under different degrees of uncertainty. These variables can be enfolded into an even simpler model of behavior that reduces it all to a function of demand. So why do you behave? In the most rudimentary sense it is because it is demanded. Naturally, when faced with demand we overtly and covertly respond in different ways. If demand is low, then we are bored and under involved, but ramping it up a bit and soon you become interested, involved, and alert. Increase it even further, and your arousal and involvement peaks, and its emotionally downhill from there as you become anxious, confused, and exhausted. All of this can be mapped to a nice smooth bell curve, where you can map how you behave and how you feel to the simple correlation between what you can do and what you must do. This bell curve, codified as the Yerkes-Dodson law, handily calculates your likely emotional state if you knew beforehand the level of demand or challenge.

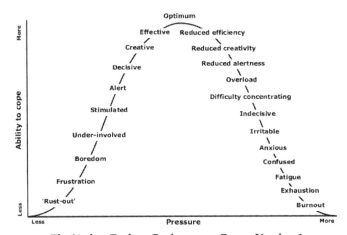

The Yerkes Dodson Performance Curve, Version 1

The problem though is that the Yerkes-Dodson law[53] has little if anything to do with Yerkes or Dodson, and may be rephrased to demonstrate correlations for many different psychological states. As the psychologist Karl Teigen put it: *In its original form as published in 1908, the law was intended to describe the relation between stimulus strength and habit-formation for tasks varying in discrimination difficultness. But later generations of investigations and textbook authors have rendered it variously as the effects of punishment, reward, motivation, drive, arousal, anxiety, tension or stress upon learning, performance, problem-solving, coping or memory; while the task variable has been commonly referred to as difficulty, complexity or novelty, when it is not omitted altogether. These changes are seldom explicitly discussed, and are often misattributed to Yerkes and Dodson themselves. The various reformulations are seen as reflecting conceptual changes and current developments in the areas of learning, motivation and emotion, and it is argued that the plasticity of the law also reflects the vagueness of basic psychological concepts in these areas.[54]*

In other words, the Yerkes-Dodson law approaches meaninglessness because it is merely a taxonomy for a lot of meanings that if patched together can result in nice smooth bell curves. Nonetheless, relationships or correlations between demand and arousal are useful, and are the stuff of the daily heuristics or rules of thumb that we use to guide our lives. However, correlations themselves may not suggest explanations, and can indeed impede or obscure them. Many of the relationships we perceive are obviously spurious because they have no conceivable explanation, and even if 'explained' by inferred forces or processes, repeat observations would dissuade us of their reliability. For example, rising hemlines may correlate with rising stock prices for a period of months, and may be explained by the conjecture that stock brokers are emotionally perked up at the sight of a more revealing female dress, but observations over the long-term view dispel them. On the other hand, other relationships not only provide strong and consistent correlations, but allow us to quickly determine explanations. For example, a day of continuous rainfall correlates with flooding, but because we know the simple metaphors of hydraulics, we can easily move from correlation to explanation by understanding how collecting rain water causes floods. Correlations are still strong when you take a few steps back and enfold a primary cause or causes into a more encompassing taxonomy or classification that may at turns reflect meanings that are clear or obscure. For example, you can say that bad weather causes flooding, but 'bad weather' suggests the causes of flooding, namely excessive rainfall. In this case, the explanation for bad weather is preserved. However, the taxonomy of demand or for arousal does not suggest its components, and in fact obscures them. That is, the independent measure of demand and the dependent measure of arousal signify disparate processes (e.g., anxiety, interest, and challenge) that denote no clearly defined constituent parts; hence the meaning or semantics of demand and arousal are vague or obscure. Of course, it can be helpful to be vague. It's simple, gets attention, makes a model that has some face validity, and it serves you well as a rule of thumb unless you want to make some specific prediction. That's when the model becomes inconsistent and fails, and it becomes incumbent to define your terms.

A Law for all Seasons

In psychology, nothing is more impressive than a bell curve. Bell curves tell you where you stand academically, socially, and psychologically. They are a swell way of graphically making an argument that hedges its bets. Thus, you can be anywhere on the curve, it just depends. Bell curves also have a faux mathematical rigor about them. Like a physical law, you change one variable and the other one changes in a proportional way. One such behavioral algorithm is the Yerkes-Dodson curve, which is mere metaphor really, as we commonly invoke the Yerkes-Dodson curve to support the hoary cliché in psychology that demand (i.e., stress) is good for you up to a point when things start going rapidly downhill (hence the bell curve).

The original Yerkes and Dodson published their hypothesis way back in the year 1908, and has little to do with the little graph you see below, which in turn doesn't have a lot of empirical support in psychology anyways, but I digress. Basically, the Yerkes Dodson curve plots performance against physical arousal, which presumably represents real discrete events that can be plotted across the X and Y axes. Thus, given an X amount of performance, you can reliably infer a Y amount of arousal, and vice versa. This is all well and good if performance and arousal are consistently defined things. The problem is, for arousal at least, it's not. What is arousal? Indeed, there are many kinds: sexual, emotional, physical. Thus, a fellow can be aroused while peeping into the girls' locker room, and aroused in a different way upon being discovered, and aroused more differently yet as he hightails it away.

Moreover, different states of arousal have different relationships to performance, and can occur separately or at the same time. Attentive alertness, as a form of arousal, increases performance as arousal increases. On the other hand, tension and attendant autonomic arousal, or anxiety, always decreases performance. Separate them both and the Yerkes-Dodson curve disappears, but combine them and out it pops. For example, a person who is highly and pleasurably aroused while climbing a mountain or creating art doesn't suffer in performance as his arousal increases, but gains in performance. On the other hand, a person who is frustrated while performing a task progressively loses his ability to perform well as anxiety increases. Nonetheless, as demand increases and decreases, these two very different types of arousal can occur simultaneously, and produce a performance curve very similar to the Yerkes-Dodson model.

As an aroused state, attentive alertness scales with the novelty or surprise of moment to moment behavior. As a function of the release of the neurochemical dopamine, touch and go events that entail continuous positive surprises (e.g. rock climbing, gambling, creative behavior) positively correlate with aroused alertness, which not only feels good but helps you think better. Thus, the bigger the positive surprise, the more alert you become, and the better your performance becomes. If, however, surprises start to trend from good to bad, alertness decreases as we become progressively more depressed, but tension and associated autonomic arousal (i.e. anxiety) increases. That is, as news moves from good to bad, arousal doesn't increase, it just changes to an entirely new form! The problem though is that positive surprises always come at the risk that things will take a decided turn for the worse, as the rock climber get stuck in a snow storm and the creative artist hits a writer's block. Thus, the cost of higher good feelings is the chance you take that a turn of fortune will turn those good feelings bad. Generally, as demand increases risk increases, and at first we can handle it and be pleasantly surprised by and are motivated by the continuous moment to moment surprise of our success. But as demand ratchets up we are more likely to experience failure, and another type of arousal, that of anxiety. Hence as demand goes up, so do performance and arousal until performance reaches a crest and arousal begins to change not in amplitude but begins changing in kind. So, the Yerkes Dodson bell curve survives, it is rather the idea that arousal does not change in kind across the level of performance that falls away.

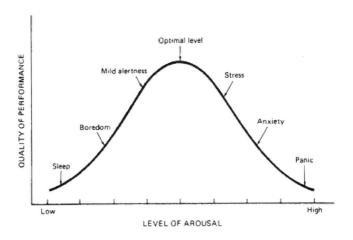

Yerkes Dodson Performance Curve, Version 2 of 200

The lesson we learn from all this is that the highest motivation or performance stands at the cusp of failure, as we are rarely motivated by the sure and thus boring thing. Unfortunately, what psychologists take from the Yerkes-Dodson curve is the wrong lesson entirely, that arousal is a monolithic and indivisible thing that does not categorically change as demand increases. In other words, the lesson that no pain equals no gain is wrong. Rather, if you have pain you will likely have no gain. For folks that are a bit wary of the school of hard knocks, this is perhaps a lesson one can get a bit excited about.

To begin defining your terms, you must first define what you are measuring, and we will start with the dependent measure of arousal. We will notice first that there are multiple ways you can be aroused. Indeed, the Yerkes-Dodson performance curve is dotted with emotional transformations from boredom and interest to anxiety and bliss. These demonstrate that for arousal, there are many distinctive emotional correlates, and the problem seems complex and near intractable. After all, our emotions are incredibly diverse, or least that is what the innumerable metaphors for emotion would hold. Yet observation provides a different perspective that our emotions are not as idiosyncratic as they seem, and represent mainly the permutations of simple and elementary processes. For the processes that underlie arousal, namely the neurological and autonomic (i.e., neuro-muscular) response to information, our argument so far has followed along these lines. However, this position is not original, and was proposed more than a hundred years ago.

Wundt Was Wight!

(with apologies to Elmer Fudd)

In 1897, Wilhelm Wundt, the founding father of experimental psychology, proposed a dimensional scheme for affect. According to Wundt: "In this manifold of feelings… it is nevertheless possible to distinguish certain different chief directions, including certain affective opposites of predominant character." Wundt identified three bipolar dimensions: (i) pleasurable versus un-pleasurable, (ii) arousing versus subduing, and (iii) strain versus relaxation. From our analysis so far, these affective states may be mapped to the activity of opioid (pleasure), dopaminergic (arousal), and neuro-muscular (strain) systems, which may in turn be mapped to information as reflected by act-outcome contingencies. Wundt proposed that these dimensions laid the foundation for emotional experience. Despite subsequent research inspired by many of Wundt's ideas (most notably in the field of psychophysics), his theory of affect had lain dormant for a century. True to his physiological training (but in contrast to his competitor and contemporary William James), Wundt assumed that affect originated in the brain and not in the peripheral body. Thus, Wundt implicitly rued the lack of technology that might allow him to track neural activity and correlate it with affect when he stated: "Which central regions are thus affected we do not know. But...the physiological substrata for all the elements of our psychological experience are probably to be found in the cerebral cortex..."[55]

Wundt's analysis was prescient, and foreshadows later findings that distinguish between the neural opioid systems that modulate physical pleasure or 'liking', the dopaminergic systems that modulate attentive arousal or 'wanting'[56], and those that modulate autonomic arousal and opioid activity as respectively elicited by muscular tension and relaxation. Emotions in other words could be spun from first principles, like the motions of a ball from an algebraic cipher, or the colors of an artist's pallet from an admixture of three primary colors. Knowing how colors are derived from the primary colors of red, green, and blue give you the color wheel, where every shade and hue can be derived from these basic colors. Similarly, Wundt's observation found illustration in 'circumplex' descriptions of emotion, wherein diverse emotional states are derived from the distinctive subjective aspect of experience, or its 'qualia'. As a modern-day exemplar of this the Feldman Barrett and Russell emotional circumplex maps emotional states such as elation, tension, boredom etc. to the intersection of concurrent primary arousal states that move on the subjective axes from unpleasant to pleasant and activation to deactivation.[57]

The problem with this emotional circumplex, as with the color wheel, is that they provide no explanation for arousal or color. So just as mapping color requires explaining color as a function of aspects of different wavelengths of light, so too does a description of primary arousal states require them to be explained, or in other words, described not just subjectively, but objectively, and refer to actual neuro-biological systems. The Feldman Barrett and Russell model maps the subjective and not objective correlates of emotional experience, and does not map out the informative characteristics of the 'demand' that elicits these responses. It is this independent measure of information, in addition to the dependent measure of arousal that must be defined. Doing so can provide the bases for an explanatory model for the states of arousal processes that comprise emotions that we argue are based upon the mundane events that comprise daily experience.

Activation

	Tense		Alert	
Nervous		y		Excited
Stressed	$-x + y$		$x + y$	Elated
Upset				Happy
Unpleasant	$-x$		x	**Pleasant**
Sad				Content
Depressed	$-x - y$		$x - y$	Serene
Bored		$-y$		Relaxed
	Fatigued		Calm	

Deactivation

[a] The letters x and y represent semantic components of core affect: x = pleasantness; y = activation (Feldman Barrett & Russell, 1998).

The cognitive representations of our day-to-day activities primarily involve decision making between multiple exclusive alternatives under varying degrees of uncertainty. These *'core appraisals'* represent moment to moment changes in the abstract (uncertainty) and functional properties (utility) of environmental contingencies that are consciously or non-consciously perceived. Parallel somatic (tension and autonomic arousal), pleasurable (opioid release due to relaxation) and activating or 'energizing' (enhanced activity of dopamine neurons) events strongly correlate with specific permutations of these core appraisals, and are 'painful' or 'pleasurable' in nature. These changes alter the importance or salience of a momentary response option and as an additive function create emergent emotional states.

The cognitive variables of *contrast* and *discrepancy* can be observed to respectively correlate with tension and activation or alertness (as defined by its neurological correspondence with the increased activity of mid-brain dopamine systems)[58] In addition, the degree of contrast, discrepancy, and the predicted utility of moment to moment responding in combination correlate with the level of tension and activation, and in their various permutations correspond with subjective emotional states.

As defined:

Contrast reflects the comparative value of two alternative means-end expectancies or response contingencies.

Discrepancy reflects moment to moment unexpected variances in the immediate predicted outcome of a behavior.

Predicted Utility reflects the value of a moment to moment response as determined by long term hedonic (e.g. food, sex, etc.) or rational value (e.g. monetary reward).

Incentive salience reflects the relative importance of moment to moment responding under a response contingency due to the utility of a response and to affective responses elicited by concurrently perceived discrepancy.

If there is a contrast between two alternative response contingencies of equal utility under certainty (i.e., little or no discrepancy in moment to moment act-outcome relationships), tension will occur, but the level of tension will vary with the predicted utility of a moment to moment response. Thus, tension will be less for low-utility choices than high. As these contingencies diverge in value, we make rational decisions to choose one of the alternatives and progressively less tension will occur. Thus, the choice between two conflicting low value alternatives (e.g. what dessert to order in a restaurant) will result in lower tension than a choice between two conflicting high value alternatives (e.g. what medical procedure to choose to treat a life-threatening condition). In addition, less tension will occur when more information is available that leads to one choice becoming more logically compelling.

The increase in dopaminergic activity due to moment-to-moment discrepancy adds another variable that increases not only the incentive salience of moment to moment responding, but also alertness (i.e., sensorimotor activation) and affective tone (i.e., a good or bad feeling). Dopamine induced activation also scales monotonically with the qualitative or informative aspects of discrepancy.[59] For example, tasks that entail moment to moment positive discrepancy (e.g. creative behavior, sporting activities, surfing the web, etc.) under circumstances wherein the incentive salience of alternative responses is relatively low will correlate with feelings of alertness/activation or 'pleasure' *and* low or non-existent tension (or low degree of discomfort or a pleasant feeling). Tasks that entail a moment to moment positive discrepancy wherein the incentive salience of alternative responses is relatively high will correlate with feelings of pleasure *and* high and/or constant tension (or high discomfort or pain). These feelings will also increase as the utility of a response increases, or in other words, we become more alert as the 'stakes' increase, and less alert as they decrease. As the incentive salience of alternative responses increases to match the increasing salience of a primary response, the level of tension and corresponding autonomic activation will increase as well, and result in a state of anxiety. Correspondingly, if the salience of a response increases as the salience of an alternative response decreases, tension will fall and activation will increase, resulting in a state of elation or ecstasy due to the combined activity of opioid (due to relaxation) and dopamine systems (due to act-outcome discrepancy).

For example, moment to moment positive discrepancy in high value sporting or creative events (e.g., a 'flow' response)[60] is marked by a feeling of energy, or 'elation' and corresponding low tension induced autonomic arousal or 'coolness under pressure' and accompanying pleasure when the salience of contrasting response options is low. However, as the salience of these options increase in value, tension becomes progressively more likely to occur both in persistence and intensity until activation and tension are continual and high, or in other words, we become anxious or stressed. In addition, as the salience of both primary and alternative response options *decreases*, activation decreases along with muscular tension, and we feel pleasurably relaxed. Finally, a predictable response option that is highly salient due primarily to its high predicted utility and contrasts with low value alternatives will often be reported as a boring or depressing experience if activation is not high enough (as embodied by the under stimulation of the dopamine system) to energize one to "want" to perform an action that is ultimately valuable (e.g. working under a piece work schedule of reward such as in an assembly line).

To illustrate how affect dynamically changes over time as a function of information and discrepancy, consider the hypothetical example of a worker in a home office (Figure 1). Waking up in the morning and accessing email, the daily news, social network postings, etc. correlates with a feeling of pleasantness (1). However, as the morning progresses, this behavior begins to contrast with other equally salient response options (her work), correlating with sustained tension (2). If these 'distractive' choices continue, the musculature will soon fatigue and be replaced by other muscular groups, creating muscular pain and a feeling of exhaustion at the end of the day. If the worker begins to cold call clients with little or no response, then she will quickly become bored (3), and may also become depressed when she recognizes that her lack of activation forestalls her obtaining her long term goals. Taking a time out from her duties by sitting quietly and barring distractive thoughts will result in relaxation (4). If she is completing a project to meet a deadline "just in time", then she will feel pleasantly alert (5). If she falls behind her task and/or is distracted by other pressing matters and thus perceives alternative irreconcilable choices or dilemmas, she will feel anxious (6).

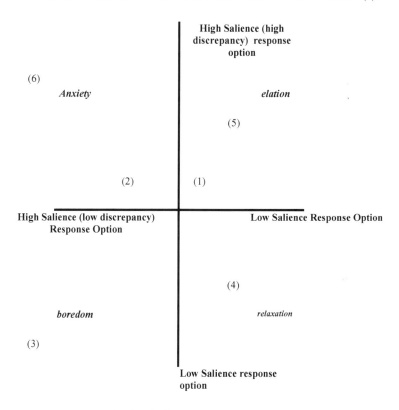

Behavioral Circumplex Model of Emotion

Emotion as a Conceptual Act

This model assumes that emotional states are additive functions of separate somatic and neurological events (tension, opioid and dopamine activity) that are highly correlated with different informative or cognitive causes (contrast, discrepancy) that are abstract properties of response contingencies. The model conforms to the Conceptual Act Model of emotion that suggests that "these emotions (often called 'basic emotions') are not biologically hardwired, but instead, are phenomena that emerge in consciousness "in the moment," from two more fundamental entities: core affect and categorization" (Wikipedia). Per this model, "core affect is a pre-conceptual primitive process, a neuro-physiological state, accessible to consciousness as a simple non-reflective feeling: feeling good or bad, feeling lethargic or energized"[61]. "Core affect is characterized as the constant stream of transient alterations in an organism's neuro-physiological state that represents its immediate relationship to the flow of changing events…. The Conceptual Act Model allows for the existence of processes that are biologically given but whose content must be learned. It considers affect as a core feature of all aspects of human psychology. Third, it relies on a situated conceptualization view of conceptual knowledge. The conceptual knowledge that is called forth to categorize affect is tailored to the immediate situation, acquired from prior experience, and supported by language"[62]. Ultimately, the difference between both models is a matter not of theory, but of semantics. Namely, with the Conceptual Act model, core affect has no clear specific or objective referent. In other words, the neuro-physiological concomitants of pain/pleasure, lethargy/energy and the elemental informative or cognitive events that correlate with these processes are not clearly defined nor are they clearly mapped to information as denoted by the flow of changing events. As a solution to this problem, high and pronounced tension and autonomic arousal are posited to represent an unpleasant state, and profound relaxation represents a pleasant state. Similarly, the high and persistent activation of dopamine systems is related to high activation and alertness, and conversely low activation of dopamine systems is related to low activation and low alertness or boredom. The graphical representation of this model parallels 'circumplex' models of affect[63] that posit that emotions are additive functions of separate affective processes that are mediated by separate causes (Figure 2).

By establishing a clear meaning for the components of affect through the clarification of their abstract cognitive or informative antecedents, neuro-physiological content, and informative consequences, the circumplex model is transformed from a descriptive account of emotion to a *predictive* account that allows behavior and affect to be clearly defined and reliably mapped to simple patterns of information that in turn denotes act-outcomes relationships or behavioral contingencies. In other words, emotions are *behavioral*, and can be described and manipulated through the simple arrangement of response contingencies.

Ultimately, this analysis validates the psychologist B.F. Skinner's original conceptualization of a radical behaviorism that mapped behavior to abstract properties of information as denoted by schedules of reinforcement or act-outcome contingencies. Whereas in his time Skinner could only map overt responses to contingencies, the resolving power of our present day observational tools allow us to map the same contingencies to the activity of affective systems in the brain (opioid and dopamine systems) as well as covert neuro-muscular activity, and provides contingency or behavior analysis with much greater predictive power and scope. Whether behavior analysts will avail themselves of this new perspective remains for the future to decide.

The Flow Experience

The Yerkes-Dodson model of arousal was of course not the only model that attempted to map emotion to demand. Consider an alternative yet similar model for yet another supposedly unique emotional state, the flow experience. Flow was coined by the psychologist Mihalyi Csikszentmihalyi[64] to describe the unique emotional state that parallels one's complete 'immersion' in a task. As described by the psychologist Daniel Goleman, "Flow is completely focused motivation. It is a single-minded immersion and represents perhaps the ultimate in harnessing the emotions in the service of performing and learning. In flow, the emotions are not just contained and channeled, but are energized and aligned with the task at hand. To be caught in the ennui of depression or the agitation of anxiety is to be barred from flow. The hallmark of flow is a feeling of spontaneous joy, even rapture, while performing a task."[65] These descriptions are of course metaphorical representations of the experience of flow, and describe what flow is like rather than what it is. Because these 'dependent' measures of flow have no empirical referent (What is the neurological equivalent of spontaneous joy for instance?), one is left with the independent or antecedent variables of demand and skill that elicit flow, which thankfully *can* be empirically defined. What is unique about these variables is that they not only map to flow experiences, but also other emotional experiences such as anxiety and boredom. Thus, Csikszentmihalyi's model does not just represent flow, but a wide range of emotional experiences. The question is, although emotion maps to demand and skill, can demand or skill be manipulated *in the moment* to elicit flow, or for that matter, any other emotion?

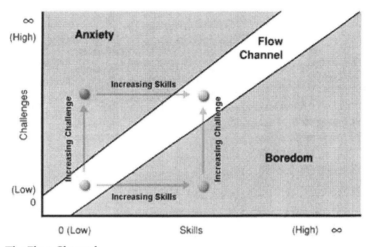

The Flow Channel

On the surface, the graphical representation of the flow channel is simple to understand. Just plot your moment-to-moment challenge against your moment to moment skill, and voila, you can predict what your emotions are going to be. For any task, the problem is that although demand moves up or down dependent upon the exigencies of the moment, skill should be relatively stable during or *within* the performance, and only change, and for the most part gradually *between* performances. Thus, one may accomplish a task that from moment to moment varies in demand, but the skills brought to that task are the same *regardless* of demand. What this means is that for any one-performance set, skill is not a variable, but a constant. That is, one cannot adjust skill against demand during performance because skill can only change negligibly *during* performance, or in other words does not move. Thus, for performance that requires any skill set, the only variable that can be manipulated *is* demand. For moment to moment behavior the adjustable variable that elicits flow is demand and demand alone. But that leaves us with figuring out what demand exactly is.

A demand may be defined as simple response-outcome contingency. Thus, if you do X, Y will occur or not occur. It is thus inferred that demand entails a fully predictable means-end relationship or expectancy. But the inference that the act-outcome expectancy is always fully predictable is not true. Although a response-outcome is fully predictable when skill overmatches demand, as demand rises to match and surpass skill, uncertainty in the prediction of a performance outcome also rises. At first, the uncertainty is positive, and reaches its highest level when a skill matches the level of demand. This represents a 'touch and go' experience wherein every move most likely will result in a positive outcome. It is here that many individuals report euphoric flow like states. Passing that, the moment-to-moment uncertainty of a bad outcome increases, along with a corresponding rise in tension and anxiety.

Momentary positive uncertainty as a logical function of the moment to moment variance occurring when demand matches skill does not translate into a predictor for flow, and is ignored in Csikszentmihalyi's model because uncertainty by implication *does not elicit affect*. Rather, affect is imputed to metaphorical concepts of immersion, involvement, and focused attention that are not grounded to any specific neurological processes. However, the fact that act-outcome discrepancy *alone* has been correlated with specific neuro-chemical changes in the brain that map to euphoric, involved, timeless[66], or immersive states, namely the activation of dopamine systems, narrows the cause of flow to abstract elements of perception rather than metaphorical aspects of performance. These abstract perceptual elements denote information, and can easily be defined and be reliably mapped to behavior.

A final perceptual aspect of demand that correlates with the elicitation of dopamine is the importance of the result or goal of behavior. Specifically, dopaminergic systems are activated by the in tandem perception of discrepancy and the predicted utility or value of result of a response contingency. The flow model maps behavior to demand and skill, but not only is skill fixed, so is the importance of the goal state that predicates demand. However, the relative importance of the goal state correlates with the intensity of affect. For example, representing an task that matches his skills, a rock climber ascending a difficult cliff would be euphoric if the moment to moment result was high, namely avoiding a fatal fall, but would be far less so if he was attached to a tether, and would suffer only an injury to his pride is he were to slip. Finally, the flow experience correlates also with a state of relaxation and the concomitant activation of opioid systems that impart a feeling of pleasure, which would also be predicted as choices in flow are singular and clear and therefore avoid perseverative cognition. It is the sense of relaxation induced pleasure and attentive arousal that constitutes the flow experience.

The flow experience, like the Yerkes-Dodson model that predates it, is not an explanatory model because it does not derive from a neurologically grounded explanation. Secondly, it is not even a very good *descriptive* model because it imputes a moment-to-moment variability in skill within a performance set that is not characteristic of *any* single performance, and because it ignores other correlations between moment to moment act-outcome discrepancy (or risk) and affect that are well demonstrated in neurological explanations of incentive motivation. For example, 'meaningful' behaviors like doing a good deed elicit dopaminergic activity because of the positive uncertainty of the *results* of behavior, not the *quality* of behavior. Thus, the positive and unexpected implications of behavior can elicit positive affect without need for a demand/skill equivalence. In other words, a rock climber can achieve high positive affect through the demand/skill match as he riskily climbs a mountain, or he can get equally affected by taking a safe straight and narrow course, motivated by the pleasant likelihood of a treasure laying at the end of the trail.

Ultimately, the flow experience purports to explain a key facet of incentive motivation through an inductive approach that misrepresents the dependent (skill) and ignores the independent variables (discrepancy) that truly map to the affective and motivational experience that is flow. In other words, as a creature of metaphor flow is good literature, but not good science because it eschews the explanatory essence *of* science.

Nonetheless, as literature can speak of hidden and unrevealed truths, the flow experience emerges from affective neuroscience, with the entailments regarding meaning and human virtue and happiness conforming with Csikszentmihalyi's own research and prescriptions, which is no small feat indeed.

References

[1] Lukskin, F. (2005) *Stress Free for Good: 10 Scientifically Proven Life Skills for Health and Happiness,* Harper Collins

[2] Wolfgang Linden; Joseph W. Lenz; Andrea H. Con (2001). Individualized Stress Management for Primary Hypertension: A Randomized Trial. *Archives of Internal Medicine* 161 (8): 1071–1080.

[3] Selye, H (1950) Stress and the general adaptation syndrome, *British Medical Journal.* (4667): 1383–92.

[4] Bromberg-Martin, E. S., Matsumoto, M., & Hikosaka, O. (2010). Dopamine in motivational control: rewarding, aversive, and alerting. *Neuron,* 68(5), 815–834.

[5] Stewart, J. (1984) Reinstatement of heroin and cocaine self-administration behavior in the rat by intracerebral application of morphine in the ventral tegmental area, *Pharmacology Biochemical Behavior,* 20, 917-923

[6] Matthews, R.T. & German, D.C. (1984) Electrophysiological evidence for excitation of rat VTA dopamine neurons by morphine, *Neuroscience,* 11, 617-625

[7] Cook, C.D., Rodefer, J.S., and Picker, M.J. (1999) Selective attenuation of the antinociceptive effects of mu opioids by the putative dopamine D3 agonist 7-OH-DPAT, *Psychopharmacology,* 144: 239-247.

[8] Marmot, M. G., Wilkinson, R. G. (2006) *Social determinants of health.* 2nd ed. Oxford University Press

[9] Squire, L. R., McConnell, S. K., Zigmond, M. J. (2003) *Fundamental neuroscience,* 2nd ed. Academic Press

[10] Saito, M., Mano, T., Abe, H., Iwase S. (1986) Responses in muscle sympathetic nerve activity to sustained hand-grips of different tensions in humans. *European Journal of Applied Physiology,* 55(5), 493-498

[11] McGuigan, F. J. (1993) *Biological Psychology: A Cybernetic Science.* New York: Prentice Hall.

[12] Malmo, R. B. (1975) *On emotions, needs, and our archaic brain.* New York: Holt, Reinhart, and Winston

[13] Jacobson, E. (1970) *Modern treatment of tense patients.* Springfield, Il: Charles C. Thomas.

[14] Gellhorn, E. & Kiely, W. F. (1972) Mystical states of consciousness: Neurophysiological and clinical aspects. *Journal of Nervous and Mental Disease*, 154, 399-405

[15] **Gellhorn, E. (1967)** *Principles of autonomic-somatic integration.* **Minneapolis: University of Minnesota Press**

[16] Drolet, G., Dumont, E.C., Gosselin, I., Kinkead, R., LaForest, S., Trottier, J. (2001) Role of endogenous opioid system in the regulation of the stress response. *Progress in neuro-psychopharmacology & biological psychiatry*, 25(4), 729-741

[17] Mercer, M. E. & Holder, M. D. (1997) Food cravings, endogenous opioid peptides, and food intake: A Review. *Appetite*, **29, 325-352**

[18] McGuigan, F. J. (1993) *Biological Psychology: A Cybernetic Science.* New York: Prentice Hall.

[19] Rahkila, P., Hakala, E. Alen, M. Salminen, K, and Laatikainen, T. (1988) Beta-endorphin and corticotropin release is dependent on a threshold intensity of running exercise in male endurance athletes. *Life Science*, 43(6): 551-558

[20] Fuss, J., Steinle, J., Bindila, L, Auer, M., Kirchherr, H., Lutz, B. and Gass, P. (2015) A runner's high depends on cannabinoid receptors in mice. *PNAS*, 112:13105-13108

[21] **Ursin, H., Eriksen, H. R. (2004) The Cognitive Activation Theory of Stress.** *Psychoneuroedocrinology*, 29, 567-592

[22] **Bechara, A. & Damasio, A. (2005) The somatic marker hypothesis: a neural theory of economic decision.** *Games and Economic Behavior*, **52(2), 336-372**

[23] **Verdejo-Garcia, A. Perez-Garcia, M. & Bechara, A. (2006) Emotion, decision making, and substance dependence: A Somatic-Marker model of addiction.** *Current Neurophamarcology*, **4(1), 17-31**

[24] Bechara, A. & Damasio, A. (2005) The somatic marker hypothesis: a neural theory of economic decision. *Games and Economic Behavior*, 52(2), 336-372

[25] **Weller, J. , Levin, I.,Shiv, B. & Bechara, A. (2007) Neural correlates of adaptive decision making for risky gains and losses.** *Psychological Science*, 15(11), 958-964

[26]Csikszentmihalyi, M. (1990) *Flow, the psychology of optimal experience*. New York: Harper Collins.

[27] Seligman, M. E. P. (1975) *Helplessness: On depression, development and death*. Freeman, San Francisco.

[28] Marr, A. J. (2006) Relaxation and Muscular Tension: A Bio-behavioristic Explanation, *International Journal of Stress Management*, 13(2), 131-153

[29] Berridge, K. (2001) Reward learning: reinforcement, incentives, and expectations. *The Psychology of Learning and Motivation*, 3, Academic Press, New York.

[30] Lundberg, U. (1999) Stress Responses in Low-Status Jobs and Their Relationship to Health Risks: Musculoskeletal Disorders. *Annals of the New York Academy of Sciences*, 896, 162-172.

[31] Hagg, G. (1991) Static Workloads and occupational myalgia- a new explanation model. In P. A. Anderson, D. J. Hobart, and J. V. Danhoff (Eds.). *Electromyographical Kinesiology* (pp. 141-144). Elsevier Science Publishers, P. V.

[32] Wursted, M., Eken, T., & Westgaard, R. (1996) Activity of single motor units in attention demanding tasks: firing pattern in the human trapezius muscle. *European Journal of Applied Physiology*, 72, 323-329

[33] Wursted, M., Bjorklund, R., & Westgaard, R. (1991) Shoulder muscle tension induced by two VDU-based tasks of different complexity. *Ergonomics*, 23, 1033-1046

[34] Lundberg, U., Forsman, M., Zachau, G., Eklo F., M., Palmerud, G., Melin, B., & Kadefors, R. (2002). Effects of experimentally induced mental and physical stress on trapezius motor unit recruitment. *Work & Stress*, 16, 166-170

[35] McEwen, B. S. (1998) Stress, adaptation, and disease: allostasis and allostatic load. *New England Journal of Medicine*, 338, 171-179

[36] Fiorillo, C., Tobler, P, & Schultz, W. (2003) Discrete coding of reward probability and uncertainty by dopamine neurons. *Science*, 299:1898-1902

[37] Berridge, K. (2007) The debate over dopamine's role in reward: the case for incentive salience. *Psychopharmacology*, 191, 391-431

[38] McGuigan, F. J. & Lehrer, P. (1993) Progressive Relaxation, Origins, Principles, and Clinical Applications. In Paul M. Lehrer (Ed.). *Principles and Practice of Stress Management*, 2nd ed. Guilford Press

[39] Berkman, E. T., Leiberman, M.D., & Gable, S.L. (2009) BIS, BAS, and response conflict: Testing predictions of the revised reinforcement sensitivity theory. *Personality and Individual Differences*, 46(5-6), 586-591

[40] Eccleston, C. & Crombez, G. (1999) Pain demands attention: a cognitive-affective model of the interruptive function of pain. *Psychological Bulletin*, 125(3), 356-366

[41] Sheppard, J. A. & McNulty, J. K. (2002) The affective consequences of expected and unexpected outcomes. *Psychological Science*, 13, 85-88

[42] Miller, N. E. (1992) Studies of fear as an acquirable drive: I. Fear as motivation and fear-reduction as reinforcement in the learning of new responses. *Journal of Experimental Psychology: General*, 121(1), 6-11

[43] Mellers, B. A., McGraw, A. P. (2001) Anticipated emotions as guides to choice. *Current Directions in Psychological Science*. 10, 201-214

[44] Miller, N. E. (1971) *Selected Papers*. Atherton, Chicago

[45] Zirpoli, T. J. (2005) *Behavior Management: Applications for teachers*. 4th ed. Saddle River, N. J.: Pearson Education

[46] Holmes, D. S. (1984) Meditation and somatic arousal reduction. A review of the experimental evidence. *American Psychologist*, 39(1), 1-10

[47] Holmes, D. S. (1988) The influence of meditation versus rest on physiological arousal: a second evaluation. In Michael A. West (Ed.) *The Psychology of Meditation*, Oxford: Clarendon Press

[48] Germer, C. K., Siegel, R. D., Fulton, P.R. (2005) *Mindfulness and Psychotherapy*. Guilford Press

[49] McGuigan, F. J. (1993) *Biological Psychology: A Cybernetic Science*. New York: Prentice Hall.

[50] Sherrington, C. S. (1909) On plastic tonus and proprioceptive reflexes. *Quarterly Journal of Experimental Psychology*, 2, 109-156

[51] Gellhorn, E. & Kiely, W. F. (1972) Mystical states of consciousness: Neurophysiological and clinical aspects. *Journal of Nervous and Mental Disease*, 154, 399-405

[52] Selye, H. (1980) *Selye's Guide to Stress Research*, New York: Van Nostrand Reinhold

[53] Yerkes RM, Dodson JD (1908). The relation of strength of stimulus to rapidity of habit-formation. *Journal of Comparative Neurology and Psychology* 18: 459–482.

[54] Teigen, K. (1994) Yerkes-Dodson, A Law for All Seasons. *Theory and Psychology* 4, 525-547

[55] Wundt, W. (1902) *Outlines of Psychology*. New York: Stanford

[56] Berridge, K., Aldridge, J. (2008) Decision Utility, the brain, and pursuit of hedonic goals, Social Cognition, 26, 621-646

[57] Barrett L. F., Russell J. (1998) Independence and bipolarity in the structure of current affect. *Journal of Personality and Social Psychology*, 74, 967–984

[58] Berridge, K. (2007) The debate over dopamine's role in reward: the case for incentive salience. *Psychopharmacology*, 191, 391-431

[59] Fiorillo, C., Tobler, P, & Schultz, W. (2003) Discrete coding of reward probability and uncertainty by dopamine neurons. *Science*, 299:1898-1902

[60] Csikszentmihalyi, M. (1990) *Flow, the psychology of optimal experience*. New York: Harper Collins.

[61] Russell, J. A. (2009) Emotion, Core Affect, and Psychological Construction. *Cognition and Emotion*, 7, 1259 - 1283

[62] Barrett, L. F. (2006) Solving the emotion paradox: Categorization and the experience of emotion. *Personality and Social Psychology Review*, 10, 20-46.

[63] Russell, J. (1980) A circumplex model of affect. *Journal of Personality and Social Psychology*, 39(6), 1161-11178

[64] Barrett L. F., Russell J. (1998) Independence and bipolarity in the structure of current affect. *Journal of Personality and Social Psychology*, 74, 967–984

[65] Goleman, D. (2006) *Emotional Intelligence*. New York: Bantam

[66] Meck, W. H. (1996) Neuropharmacology of timing and time perception, *Cognitive Brain Research*, (3)3-4, 227-242